And others, Kent and Co.

The Guildhall of the City of London

Together with a Short Account of its Historic Associations, and the Municipal Work

Carried on therein

And others, Kent and Co.

The Guildhall of the City of London
Together with a Short Account of its Historic Associations, and the Municipal Work Carried on therein

ISBN/EAN: 9783337249311

Printed in Europe, USA, Canada, Australia, Japan

Cover: Foto ©Andreas Hilbeck / pixelio.de

More available books at **www.hansebooks.com**

The Guildhall

.. of the ..

City of London.

Together with a short Account of
Its historic Associations,
And the Municipal Work
Carried on therein.

Printed by order of
The Corporation of London,
Under the direction of
The City Lands Committee.

SECOND EDITION.

And Compiled
By John James Baddeley,
Chairman of the Committee, 1898.

Price:

2/6 NET.

London:
SIMPKIN, MARSHALL, HAMILTON, KENT & Co., Ltd.
1899.

PRINTED BY EDEN FISHER & COMPY.,
6, 7 & 8, CLEMENT'S LANE & 96-97, FENCHURCH STREET, E.C.

CONTENTS.

PREFACE.

THE Corporation of the City of London has, during the past half century, published, chiefly under the superintendence of its Library Committee, a series of volumes compiled from its own archives, which extend back for more than six hundred years. These volumes deal with the City's history, its ceremonials and its ancient historical buildings; among these may be mentioned for our present purpose, Riley's 'Memorials of London Life,' 'The Ceremonial Book,' 'London's Roll of Fame,' Welch's 'Guildhall Library and its Work,' Price's 'Historical Account of the Guildhall,' and Dr. Sharpe's 'London and the Kingdom.' The present book has been almost entirely compiled from the above-named works. The formal description of the Guildhall has been taken, for the most part, from Price's 'Account,' and the historical facts rehearsed in the short summary of the City's history from Dr. Sharpe's volumes ; entire passages have been taken from both, and the compiler desires to make all due acknowledgement of the great assistance these books have been to him in the production of this volume.

Although this work is chiefly intended as a Guide to the Guildhall, it is thought that the visitor would consider it incomplete, were not some information afforded respecting the more important events that have taken place within its walls, as well as the ceremonies and public functions, that are to be witnessed there in these days. A summary of its historic past has been therefore added, together with a short history of the Mayoralty, and the Courts of Aldermen and Common Council.

It is also thought that a short account of the work now being carried on by the Court of Common Council in the Government of the "one square mile" will be of interest, not only to the citizens, but, also to the stranger who comes within the City's boundaries.

J.J.B.

GUILDHALL, 1899.

THE . . . .

GUILDHALL

OF THE CITY OF LONDON.

The Historic Past.

THE student of the history of the City of London, its
Mayors, Aldermen, Common Council and Citizens, will
be easily able to conjure up visions of some of the many
stirring National and Civic events, that have taken place
within the historic walls of Guildhall, and which history, when
known, may well cause a thrill of pride to swell in the breast
of the most ordinary matter-of-fact citizen of the present day.

Truly and eloquently did Sir Walter Besant (London's
modern historian) describe the City (with its centre at Guildhall) as the protectress of freedom, when, in a recent public
address, he said : " This principle—the necessity of freedom
—was handed down from father to son ; it became the
religion of the citizens ; they proclaimed it and fought for
it ; they won it, and lost it ; they recovered part of it, and
lost it again. At last they won it altogether, and, in winning
it, they gained a great deal more than they had contemplated
or hoped for. They won for their descendants, they won for
every town where the English tongue is spoken, the rights
of free men in free cities, the rights of the individual, the
rights of property." And shall it not also be said that the
spirit of freemen which animated our illustrious predecessors
still animates many of the citizens of the present day.

Well has Mr. Loftie written in his book on London (" Historic Towns " series) that " It would be interesting to go over all the recorded instances in which the City of London interfered directly in the affairs of the Kingdom, such a survey would be a History of England as seen from the windows of the Guildhall " ; and Mr. Price in his historical account of the Guildhall writes, " The true history of the Guildhall is to be based on the numerous traditions and interesting associations by which it is connected with the most important Corporation in the world. The stirring episodes, religious, political, and social, with which this Hall has been associated for many centuries, clothe it with a far deeper interest than could any mere technical description of its walls, its masonry, the painted glass and sculpture, with which it is adorned."

Let us then, take our stand in this Guildhall, so enthusiastically spoken of, and allow our thoughts and imagination to revert to the time of the Conquest. We see the citizens strong enough to make terms with the Norman invader, and receive at his hands a Charter by which their liberties and power of self-government are guaranteed. In the contest between Stephen and the Empress Matilda (1135-1153) we see the citizens holding, as it were, the balance. Richard, Cœur-de-Lion, is assisted by the City, and we can picture his martial figure striding at times through the Hall. The citizens, in 1215, are lending their help to the Barons in wresting from the reluctant John the great Charter of England's liberties, and in return, the grateful Barons make provision for the preservation of the liberties of the City. Fitz-Walter, the leader of the Barons, and the Mayor of the City are both among those specially appointed to see the terms of the Charter strictly carried out.

We cannot linger over the almost continuous fight between the citizens and the Plantagenet kings in defence of the City's liberties and charters, but the citizens are loyal, for on receiving the news in a letter from Queen Isabel (1312) announcing the birth of Edward, afterwards the Third, at Windsor, they held high festival for a week, and on the last day of rejoicing "The Mayor, richly costumed, and the Aldermen, arrayed in like suits of robes, with the Drapers, Mercers, and Vintners, in costumes, rode on horseback to Westminster, there made offering, and then returned to the Guildhall which was excellently well tapestried and dressed out. There they dined; and after dinner went in carols, throughout the City, all the rest of the day and great part of the night." This Edward of Windsor on succeeding to the throne, is popular, and by the City's assistance in men and money is chiefly enabled to prosecute his wars in France; gaining the memorable victories of Crecy and Poictiers. Just before Crecy the citizens are in a state of alarm at the prospect of an immediate attack by the French, and protect the Guildhall by "Guns wrought of latten mounted on teleres, and charged with powder and pelletts of lead." On his return, the Mayor entertains at a grand banquet the King, and the Kings of France, Scotland, Denmark and Cyprus (1363). The citizens' influence is chiefly instrumental in deposing Edward's grandson, the weak and uncertain Richard; the articles accusing him of misgovernment are drawn up and publicly read in Guildhall (1399). We hear the Mayor saying, "Let us apparel ourselves and go and receive the Duke of Lancaster since we agreed to send for him." And, as Henry IV., son of 'time-honoured Lancaster,' he is fairly popular, although again and again he holds the charter to ransom.

Next Henry of Monmouth appears on the scene, and we may picture that brilliant gathering assemble in our new Guildhall, not yet completely finished, when the King's three brothers John, Duke of Bedford, Humphrey, Duke of Gloucester (the "good Duke Humphrey"), Edward, Duke of York, with the Archbishop of Canterbury, the Bishop of Winchester, and others, come to confer with the Mayor, as to what

assistance is to be rendered the King in his proposed claim to
the crown of France. But now arises a question of precedence
—the Mayor, as the King's representative in the City, claims to
occupy the centre seat—in other words to take the chair, and
his claim is allowed, thus making a precedent which future
Mayors are to uphold. Visions of the citizens' enthusiasm float
around, when the news of the glorious victory of Agincourt
on St. Crispin's day is announced (1415), just as the newly
elected Mayor is being sworn into office,—of " the solemn
pilgrimage of the Mayor, Aldermen and Commonalty, from
Guildhall on foot to Westminster, for the purpose of making
humble thanks to the Almighty and His saints, especially
St. Edward the Confessor, for the joyous victory." Later on, at
the termination of the war with France, the King and
Queen are entertained in the Guildhall, and we picture
Whittington, to the astonishment and delight of the King,
throwing into the fire bonds given by the King, stated to be of
the value of £60,000, and we hear Henry's exclamation,
" Happy is the King to have such a subject," and Whittington's
courtly rejoinder, " Rather, happy is the subject to have such a
King." Henry passes away and his infant son succeeds him.
Guildhall is finished, a building destined to receive and to
welcome generations of England's greatest men, and to witness
events of vital importance to the City, to England, and to the
world. Within a few years, Jack Cade and his Kentish
followers are in possession of the City, and are holding mock
trials in the Guildhall, where they sentence to death Sir James
Fiennes, Lord Say and two others, carry the sentences into
execution in Chepe, and set up the heads on London Bridge,
Cade's own head shortly joining them (1450).

Later on, we see many meetings of the Common Council,
for the purpose of aiding Henry of Monmouth's son, but, weary
at last of his weakness and favouritism, it welcomes the Duke
of York to the City, acknowledges his title to the crown,

and on his death at Wakefield Green, proclaims his son, King, as Edward IV. Popular in the early part of his reign, and the darling of the citizens, who supply his needs again and again, we may picture him paying the Guildhall frequent visits. On his death, we see the Duke of Buckingham attempting to induce the citizens to petition the crafty Gloucester to accept the crown, and then returning to his treacherous master with the news, " The citizens are mum, they say not a word." On Richard's death on Bosworth Field, Henry Tudor receives a hearty welcome from the City, and great rejoicings are held on his marriage with Elizabeth of York (1485), as happily ending the disastrous Wars of the Roses.

Our first glimpse of the Eighth Henry is when, as a boy of seven, he receives from the citizens a pair of gilt goblets ; and we listen to his youthful words of gratitude: " Fader Maire, I thank you and your Brethren here present of this greate and kynd remembraunce which I trist in tyme comyng to deserve. And for asmoche as I can not give unto you according thankes, I shall pray the Kynges Grace to thank you, and for my partye I shall not forget yoɾ kyndnesse."

In later years, we see this boy, who had returned such a gentle reply, and who hoped not merely to deserve, but who promised not to forget their kindness, transformed into a Royal despot, constantly at variance with the citizens. We may picture to ourselves in 1529 (Ralph Dodmer, Mayor) the first of the recorded Banquets on Lord Mayor's day, " with the Mayor's Court boarded and hung with cloth of Arras for the occasion," one table set apart for peers of the realm, at the head of which sits the new Lord Chancellor (Sir Thomas More), and at the bottom the Lords Berkeley and Powis, at either side of the table more peers, among whom are the Dukes of Norfolk and Suffolk, the one, the Treasurer, and the other, the Marshal of England, Sir Thomas Grey Marquis of Dorset, the Earl of Oxford the High Chamberlain, and the Earl of Shrewsbury Lord Steward

of England, Tunstal Bishop of London, and Sir Thomas
Boleyn, whose daughter Anne is shortly to experience the peril
of sharing Henry's throne. Scenes other than banquets rise
to the mind's eye—we see Anne Askew arraigned in the
Guildhall for "speaking against the sacrament of the altar," and
condemned to be burnt alive as a heretic at Smithfield. Yet, at
the same period, in this same Guildhall of ours, we are pleased
to picture grave citizens pacing the floor, full of pious schemes
for the advancement of learning, which resulted in the
establishment of the world-famed schools of the Mercers, St.
Paul's, the Merchant Taylors, and others in the City ; while
natives of the provinces, who had been successful as merchants
in the City, were founding, in the place of their birth, schools
such as Reading, Bristol, Drayton, Oundle, Tonbridge, and
Bedford—centres destined, in years to come, to produce a
more tolerant spirit throughout the land.

Their example is followed by the mild and gentle boy
King, Edward VI., who still further encourages learning,
while we see his Uncle, the Protector Somerset, in his eager-
ness to raise and furnish his stately mansion in the Strand,
borrowing and carrying away from the Guildhall Library,
several cartloads of books, the noble gift of Whitington and
Carpenter, which are destined never to be returned. In the
early struggle between the Protector and the Lords of the
Council, then in possession of the King's person, we hear the
Common Council at Guildhall promise "that they will, to the
uttermost of their wills and powers, maintain and defend the
King's person." During the later years of Edward's reign, we see
the citizens busily engaged in laying a proper foundation for
the management of the hospitals they have acquired—viz., St.
Bartholomew's for the sick poor, St. Thomas's for the indigent,
aged and infirm, Bridewell for the lazy and vagabond,
Bethlem for the mentally afflicted—and receiving permission
from the King, at the suggestion of Bishop Ridley, to set apart

what remained of Grey Friars, as Christ's Hospital, for the
education and support of fatherless and helpless children. To
consolidate this great work, the King, on his death bed, grants
a Charter of Incorporation to the Mayor, Aldermen, and
Commonalty, as Governors of these Royal Hospitals in the
City. In a letter to the Mayor, Sir Richard Dobbs, Bishop
Ridley writes, " O Dobbs, Dobbs, Alderman and Knight, thou in
thy year didst win my heart, for evermore, for that honourable
act, that most blessed work of God, of the erection and setting
up of Christ's Holy Hospitals and truly religious houses which
by thee, and through thee, were begun." Mary Tudor has
not long been on the throne when we witness the trial of
the aged Cranmer, the youthful Lady Jane Grey (she
" that wolde a been qwene"), her husband, and two of her
husband's brothers, who plead guilty and are condemned to
death. Three months after, we see the Queen (with Wyatt,
in open rebellion, in Southwark), full of the courage of her
family, " addressing a spirited harangue to the assembled
citizens," in the Guildhall, asking and receiving at their hands
loyal assistance—which she afterwards repaid with the fires of
Smithfield. Sir Nicholas Throckmorton stands his trial in
Guildhall for being implicated in Wyatt's rebellion. The trial
is remarkable for the display of intellectual power of his
advocates, and for the verdict of the Jury, in opposition to the
wishes of the Queen, which costs them imprisonment and fine.

The glorious reign of Elizabeth has now commenced
(1558), and from the Guildhall can be heard and seen signs of
rejoicing. The Guildhall is alive and astir with the
merchant adventurers, whose minds are deeply engaged in
plans for the extension of trade wherever they can set foot
in a world for the most part as yet unknown; or, as Kingsley
says, " pick the lock of the New World." We catch glimpses
of Sir Thomas Gresham pondering how he may best carry out
his father's scheme for founding a " Burse " or Exchange, for

the use of the rising merchants, and how he may best arrange his noble scheme for a college ; of the famous Lord Mayor, Edward Osborne, whose descendant (the present Duke of Leeds), three hundred years later, is now renewing the ancient family connection with City life ; of Sheriff Spencer, the wealthy Clothworker ; of Martin Frobisher and of Humphrey Gilbert, both residents close by, in Cripplegate Without ; of John Hawkins, and of Walter Raleigh, the friend of all adventurers. Early in April, 1588, the Common Council assemble with grave and troubled, but courageous looks, knowing full well that England's time of trial has come, and agree to furnish and fully equip for war, sixteen of the largest and best merchant ships that can be found in the Thames, and four pinnaces to attend on them ; and we again see them on that eventful Saturday, when an engagement with the Spaniard is expected, obeying the precept of the Lord Mayor (Sir George Bond) to attend church, " in order that humble and hearty prayers might be offered to Almighty God by preaching and otherwise, as the necessity of the times required."

One might ponder for long, over the causes which led to the City's prosperity, during the reign of the last and greatest of the Tudors, but we must travel on to Stuart times and picture the first of that race on the English throne. We see him inducing the citizens to assist with men and money in the plantation of Ulster, which is effected after much protracted negotiation and a considerable expenditure of City's cash. Assistance is also given, at his suggestion, to the Virginia Company, which carried out successfully Raleigh's idea of colonies over the sea. But these outside projects drain the supplies which were needed for home uses. The New River Act for supplying the City with water has been obtained. But the City funds are low, and, in consequence, its powers are made over to Hugh Myddelton, who, by selling to the King one half of the shares, is, at the cost of his personal fortune, able to complete this much-needed work, which in the future is to make its possessors " rich beyond the dreams of avarice."

On the proposed Royal alliance with their ancient enemy of Spain, we can imagine the bold and independent City apprentices assembling around the Guildhall, full of contempt for their haughty foe, and venting their feelings against its representative, Gondomar, who, upon giving directions to the Mayor, is met with the reply, " It is not to you that I have to give an account for the government of this City." The King comes with a threat to place a garrison in the City and withdraw the Charter, but, on second thoughts, and becoming calmer, returns with "divers Lords of the Council, and scolds the Mayor and Aldermen for their misgovernment and for the illcarriage of the rude sort of people."

We have witnessed the citizens, in the reign of Great Queen Bess, freely giving their aid, in repelling from these shores, the attempted invasion of the foreigner, we now see them doing their best to defend the liberties of their country against the attempts of an arbitrary monarch.

Charles is now on the throne, and in an hour of need (November, 1641), pays his first visit to the City ; a banquet is given in his honour, the cost defrayed out of the Chamber, the Mayor and Recorder receive the honour of Knighthood, and to show still more clearly his gratitude for the brilliant reception given him, he confers on the two Sheriffs and five of the Aldermen the same dignity. But, gratifying as these favours may be to some, a deeper issue lay below. Were there any real checks on the Monarch's personal authority, or were there not ? Three months later, this question came to the front, his officers having failed to arrest the five members (Pym, Hampden, Holles, Hazelrigg, and Strode), the King proceeds to the House of Commons to demand their arrest. Looking round, and not seeing them present, he asks the Speaker "Do you see any of them?" to which the Speaker, with due obeisance to the King, answers "May it please your Majesty, I have neither eyes to see nor tongue to speak in this place, but as the House is pleased to direct me, whose servant I am here." Foiled thus in the House, and hearing that the five members had taken refuge in the City, the King, accompanied by his retinue, presents himself next day, before the assembled Court of Common Council, and demands that the five members, who he says, are "lurking in the City," shall be delivered to him. Ominous silence reigns, which shortly afterwards is broken by a cry, " Parliament, privileges of Parliament!" from some, and "God bless the King!" from others. This is all the answer vouchsafed him ; on leaving the Council Chamber the same cries greet him in Guildhall itself. He invites himself to dine with one of the Sheriffs, whom he knows to be the least favourable to him, and leaves the City, to which he is destined never to return. The Council continue sitting, and humbly desire his Majesty to take steps for the redress of certain grievances, and also request him not to proceed against the five members.

Imagination may run riot in thinking of the meetings in the Courts of Aldermen, of Common Council, and of the Citizens, in Common Hall during the next few eventful years ; the citizens, for the most part full of energy in the Parliamentary cause, occasionally wavering, but, on the whole, requiring very little inducement to keep firm. The fate of King and Parliament is in their hands. We picture to ourselves deputations from both Houses of Parliament— Cromwell among them—waiting upon the Common Council, sometimes with thanks for prompt assistance in raising additional regiments of trained bands, sometimes asking for a supply of arms for the use of the Parliamentary forces, and at times begging for money to carry on the war.

At a specially convened Common Hall, in 1644, Vane, Warwick, Essex, Pembroke, and Holles, thank the assembled liverymen for past services, and exhort them to be firm for the future. We see the Common Council taking active steps to relieve Gloucester, at that time besieged by the king, and sending forward several regiments, supplied with cannon, to its relief. This is effected, and the City claims to have contributed much, in this "turning point in the war." We may picture the pride and enthusiasm with which the Common Council in their Guildhall receive the news from Newbury fight, that their trained bands had stood their ground, "like so many stakes," against the charges made by the fiery Rupert's royalist cavalry. Clarendon himself says, "They behaved themselves to wonder, and were in truth the preservation of that army, that day." By-and-bye this Parliament becomes only a skeleton of its former self, and the real power is now wielded by the newly-modelled and now dictatorial army ; and new demands, on behalf of the army are made on the City, much as they had been made under former Kings. Because of delay in providing moneys demanded, and as a menace to the citizens, the Mayor, Sir John Gayer of "lion sermon" fame), one of the Sheriffs, and three Aldermen were ordered, on a specious pretence, to the Tower, and on disputing the jurisdiction of the *now* House of Lords the Mayor and Aldermen were heavily fined, but on the Commons finding that the attitude of the citizens was still wavering, the prisoners (while the enemy was at the gates) were discharged without trial, once more showing that, in an important crisis, the feeling of the City has to be reckoned with. The citizens do not forget the threats and insults they have recently suffered. We hear bitter words spoken of the Army ; a Royalist reaction is in the air ; yet the general feeling of distrust in Charles's promises is a barrier to every agreement. At his trial we see five Aldermen and two wealthy citizens named on the Commission. Two of the Aldermen and the two citizens sit at the trial—but only the two latter

B

sign the death warrant, for which they suffered in after years. The long struggle being at last ended, the City now entertains, first, the Commons, and then the Council of State and other High Officers, and, later on, distinguished leaders of the Parliamentary Army. Fairfax and Cromwell they present with plate, to the value of £1,412 15s. We see Cromwell again fêted by the City after Worcester, and on being proclaimed Lord Protector ; and we hear with unfeigned sorrow of his death—the death of the greatest Englishman of the age—on 3rd September, 1658, his "fortunate day," the anniversary of Dunbar and Worcester.

His son Richard is proclaimed, but he has not his father's genius, and whispers are soon heard in Guildhall of a restoration of the old *régime*. Monk makes his appearance on the scene, and takes up his quarters in the City, much to the chagrin of the Council of State. We see him feeling the pulse of the citizens, who now begin to speak freely of the instability "of present arrangements," and some, even of a restoration. The Common Council, in touch with the rising feeling, is now anxious to put itself in a proper attitude, and to vindicate its action throughout the late troubles.

It is now May, 1660, the Common Council are appointing sixteen Commissioners to wait on the new King at the Hague, who receives them graciously, and confers the honour of knighthood upon those members who are not already knighted. Charles II., under conditions believed by the citizens to be real, is now "come to his own again," and proclaimed King by the Lord Mayor "in a new crimson velvet gown specially provided for the occasion." In July, the Guildhall witnesses scenes far different from those it has lately been accustomed, for Charles, his Court and his Parliament, are dining with the Lord Mayor and citizens, and receiving, at his Lordship's hands, "a welcome cupp, according to the usual custome," as a token of loyalty and duty. This entertainment seems to give the King a taste for the City's hospitality, for, in later years, he is here again and again.

In 1663, we picture a Lord Mayor's Banquet with Samuel Pepys as a guest, who thus lucidly describes his experience : "We went up and down to see the tables, where, under every salt, there was a bill of fare, and at the end of the table the persons proper for the table. Many were the tables, but none in the Hall but the Mayor's and Lords of the Privy Council that had napkins or knives, which was very strange. We went into the Buttry and there stayed and talked, and then into the Hall again, and there wine was offered and they drunk, I only drinking some hypocras, which do not break my vowe, it being, to the best of my present judgment, only a mixed compound drink, and not any wine ; if I am mistaken, God forgive me ! but I hope, and do think, I am not. . . . By-and-by, about one o'clock, before the Lord Mayor come into the Hall, from the room where they were first led into, the Lord Chancellor (Archbishop before him), with the Lords of the Council and other Bishopps, and they to dinner. Anon comes the Lord Mayor, who went up to the Lords and then to the other tables to bid welcome ; and so all to dinner. I set . . . at the merchant strangers' table where ten good dishes to a messe, with plenty of wine of all sorts, of which I drunk none ; but it was very unpleasing that we had no napkins nor change of trenchers, and drunk out of earthen pitchers and wooden dishes. . . . The dinner, it seems, is made by the Mayor and two Sheriffs for the time being, the Lord Mayor paying one half and they the other."

Two years after (1665) there is no feasting in the City The plague is raging and many thousands of its citizens have perished. The Guildhall has fallen upon evil times, for, in the following year, we must again picture a scene of desolation, this time of another character. No time to linger here now. The building, with all its historic memories, is placed in the midst of a sea of fire. The roof is alight and the worst is feared. Yet the " horrid, malicious, bloody flame," as Pepys calls it, burns itself out without serious injury to the walls. But public business, although impossible here, must be carried on, so a remove is made to Gresham House in Bishopsgate Street, from which the Common Council issues its orders for the Guildhall to be cleared of its debris, and the City's records (fortunately uninjured) to be removed to Gresham House, there to remain in charge of the Town Clerk. Although not now from the Guildhall itself, we see the citizens bestirring themselves in the rebuilding of their city. This is no light task, for around us are seen the ruins of 13,200 houses, many of the City Companies' halls, and 89 parish churches. Wren, the great architect, submits a plan for the re-arrangement of the streets, but, handsome and useful as such might have been, to carry it out in its entirety is found to be impracticable. A certain amount of re-modelling takes place, and, from the still roofless Guildhall, we see the new approach from Cheapside, called, in honour of his Majesty, " King Street." Wren examines the Guildhall and finds that the walls are almost uninjured, and three years after places thereon a roof, it is said, intended only to be temporary, though destined to remain for nearly 200 years. The Council Chamber is again fitted for use, the work resumed in its former quarters, and we are again able to take our position in the Hall and watch current events. In 1672, the portraits of the twenty-two Judges, who have just completed their work in defining the boundaries of properties, and settling disputes in re-building, are ordered to be hung on the walls of the Guildhall, and in the same year the Prince of Orange (afterwards William III) is handsomely entertained by the City, at the King's request. During the remainder of the so-called 'Merry Monarch's' reign, there is constant friction and strife between the King and the City, for although the latter had, in a very great degree, been instrumental in his restoration, it suffered more at his

hands, than at those of any of his predecessors. In a dispute as
to whether the City was going beyond its chartered powers, a
Quo Warranto was issued in 1682 ; and although the citizens, as
has been their wont, boldly fight for their Charter and their
chartered rights of electing their own Mayor, Aldermen, and
Common Council—there is no election of the last-named for six
years, and the Lord Mayor and Aldermen are appointed by the
King. His brother and successor, James, maintains the same
policy, until circumstances compel him to see the folly of
alienating the citizens ; he is then ready to make concessions
and restore their Charter, and does so, but too late to save his
throne. The King has fled from London (1688). A meeting is
held in the Guildhall, fraught with consequences of the greatest
importance both to the City and the Kingdom. A number
of the Lords spiritual and temporal come to the Guildhall,
as to "a place of security," the better to take measures,
and consult for the commonweal. They inform the Court
of Aldermen of the King's flight, and then retire into the
"gallery adjoining the Council Chamber," where they draw up
a declaration containing, in effect, their resolution to assist the
Prince of Orange, (whose landing in England had caused King
James to take to flight), in "maintaining the religion, the
rights, and liberties which had been invaded by Jesuitical
Counsels." At a meeting immediately after, the Common
Council implore the Prince's protection, and promise him a
hearty welcome to the City, while the Court of Lieutenancy
assure his Highness that measures had been taken for preserving
the peace of the City till he should arrive. The Prince and
his Consort are crowned in April, and on the next Lord
Mayor's Day, witness the Show from Cheapside, and, in the
evening are, with the members of both Houses and High
Officers of State, entertained at a Banquet in the Guildhall.

The decision in the *Quo Warranto* proceedings is reversed,
and we see the citizens restored to the full enjoyment of all

their ancient rights and privileges, and anxious to do all in their power to strengthen the position of their new Sovereign, who, in return, is most gracious, and honours them with his presence on Lord Mayor's Day, 1692. William and Mary pass away, and good Queen Anne reigns. On the first Lord Mayor's Day after her accession, she attends the usual banquet, and, as an acknowledgment of the City's welcome, she confers the honour of knighthood on several distinguished citizens, and does not forget the claims of " Mr. Eaton," Linen Draper of Cheapside, from the windows of whose house she had witnessed the pageant pass.

We now see that famous General, John, Duke of Marlborough, frequently entertained by the City, and are able to view twenty-six standards and sixty-three colours, taken at Ramillies, brought in great state into the City and displayed on the walls of the Guildhall.

Queen Anne is dead, to the great grief of the citizens. George of Hanover succeeds, and, as has become the custom, attends the first Lord Mayor's Day Banquet after his accession. His successor—the second of that name—together with the Queen, the great officers of State and a large number of the nobility, continues the custom (1727).

The Rebellion of '45 causes for a time much consternation in Guildhall, and we see the citizens expressing their thankfulness at their deliverance, by unanimously resolving to present to the Duke of Cumberland, the " Freedom of the City " in a gold box, both for his " magnanimous behaviour against the rebels as well as for his vigilant care in protecting the City in a late time of imminent danger." Towards the close of this reign, we see the " Freedom of the City " conferred on one, whose name is still held by his country in the highest esteem—William Pitt, afterwards Earl of Chatham, "who had done so much to restore the ancient reputation of the British Empire." The third George succeeds (1760), and attends (following the custom of his predecessors) the first Lord Mayor's Banquet after his accession. Pitt also is there, and is received with even greater acclamation than the King himself. We next see the citizens entering on a conflict partly with the King,—who was suspected of trying to restore again, in political matters, the personal ascendancy of the Sovereign,—and partly with the House of Commons, for the freedom of the electors to choose their own representatives, and for the liberty of the Press. We see them (1764) conferring the " Freedom of the City " on Chief Justice Pratt for deciding that general warrants were illegal. The citizens support Wilkes, because they believe him to be fighting at the first, a battle against personal government, and afterwards in defence of the rights of the people to elect their representatives. In 1770, Lord Mayor Beckford, after presenting an address to the King from the City and receiving his Majesty's unfavourable reply, remonstrates with him on the indifference and disregard with which the citizens' addresses to the King had been received. On hearing this, the Earl of Chatham observed, " *The spirit of Old England* spoke that never-to-be-forgotten day." In the following year, we see Brass Crosby, the Lord Mayor, Member for Honiton in the House of Commons, and Alderman Oliver, a representative of the City in that House, sent, by order of the Commons, to the Tower, because, as magistrates of London, they had discharged two printers who had publicly reported the debates in the House, contrary to its rule, and who had disobeyed the summons to appear at its bar. We hear the shouts of the populace greeting them as the ' people's friends, the guardians of the City's rights and of the nation's liberties.' It is worthy of note that these debates have ever since been regularly reported.

During the war with the American Colonies, we may fancy ourselves present at a meeting of the Livery in Common Hall, in support of the claims of the Colonists, and hear them draw up a " respectful but solemn warning against the fatal policy pursued by the King's Ministers toward the American Colonies," in which they state that the measures which the Government have recently adopted are " big with all consequences which can alarm a free and commercial people," and, later on, the Common Council passes a resolution that a humble address and petition be presented to his Majesty praying him " to suspend hostilities, and adopt such conciliatory measures as might restore union, confidence and peace, to the whole Empire." If the King will but listen to the prayer of his faithful citizens, the American Colonies will remain with us loyal and united ; but no, the King's eyes are " holden," and Providence decrees that the ' United States of America ' shall be founded and become the wonder of the world.

We see " Halls " and Common Council supporting the youthful Minister, Pitt, the son of their favourite, Chatham, and hail, with enthusiasm, the energy with which the citizens enrol themselves as Volunteers, when invasion is threatened by the " Scourge of Europe." We picture, in 1805, Pitt, though broken down in health by the burden he cheerfully bore, attending, at a cost of much personal suffering, the Lord Mayor's Banquet, and when the Lord Mayor, in proposing his health, styles him the Saviour of Europe, we may hear his short and modest reply, " I return you many thanks, my Lord Mayor, for the honour you have done me, but Europe is not to be saved by any single man. England has saved herself by her exertions, and will, I trust, save Europe by her example." These were the last words he ever spoke in public.

Two years later, we again witness the renewal of the struggle, both for the freedom of speech and for the freedom of the Press. Sir Francis Burdett is committed to the Tower by order of the House of Commons, for questioning the right of the House to commit a man to prison, for proposing to discuss in a Debating Society, the proceedings of that House. The Livery assemble in Common Hall to take into consideration "the alarming assumption of privilege, by the Honourable the House of Commons, of arresting and imprisoning, during pleasure, the people of England, for offences cognizable in the usual Courts of Law," and thank Sir Francis Burdett for having upheld the right of freedom of speech.

This meeting of Common Hall,—the forerunner of many during succeeding years,—renews the claim for reform—first put forward after Wilkes' return for Middlesex, constantly urged by Common Halls up to Pitt's unsuccessful attempt to realize it in 1785, and then for a time stilled by the excesses of the French Revolution,—which led, in 1832, to such an extension of the franchise, and such a redistribution of seats, as gave the nation in general a real and effective control over the Government of the day. We see both the Common Council and the Common Halls presenting strongly-worded addresses with this end in view, and the long struggle only ceases, when the Bill of Earl Grey, for Reform, has passed both Houses. The victory is celebrated in Guildhall, when Lord Grey and Lord Althorp are admitted as the fellow " freemen " of those who had fought so long for victory. At a specially-arranged banquet in honour of those who, by their exertions, had contributed to this great result, we hear Lord Grey paying a deserved tribute to the City's influence in the commercial world, its loyalty to the constitution, and its love of freedom, "never more conspicuously manifested " than during recent events.

During the latter years of this agitation, the citizens are active in supporting in their Guildhall the repeal of the Test Acts, the demand for Catholic Emancipation, and, even when rejoicing at the downfall of Napoleon, careful that the noble work of abolishing the trade in slaves, which was secured by the perseverance of William Wilberforce, should not be undone.

Turning one's thoughts away from politics, we see the City, after the occupation of Paris, and the overthrow of Napoleon (1814), entertaining at Guildhall, at a magnificent banquet, a brilliant assembly—the Czar of Russia, the King of Prussia, the newly-restored scion of the Bourbons, Louis XVIII., the Prince Regent, and a host of other distinguished personages. In a few weeks there follows another gathering, scarcely less brilliant, to do honour to him, who, as Commander of the British forces, had done more than any other, to stay the victorious career of Napoleon—the Duke of Wellington. The opportunity is taken of presenting him with the "Freedom of the City" (in a gold box), which he had hitherto been unable "to take up," as well as with the sword of honour already voted him. We see further banquets and entertainments given in keeping with the wealth and dignity of the City, in honour of Royal personages, of illustrious statesmen, and of brave warriors; we see men, for ever famous in the world's history, welcomed here, and receiving the highest gift the citizens can bestow—the honorary freedom of the City; an honour, which we hear the recipients saying, "they esteem equal to any honour that may be placed upon them." Besides those already mentioned, we have welcomed to Guildhall statesmen and philanthrophists—Peel, Brougham, Russell, Clarkson, Livingstone, Disraeli, Gladstone, Salisbury, Dufferin, and Shaftesbury; commanders by sea and by land—Nelson, Hood, Jervis, Howe, Duncan, Abercrombie, Wellington, Hill, Hardinge, Gough, Williams of Kars, Colin Campbell, Outram, Wolseley, Roberts, Kitchener, and many others.

Following the custom of many of her predecessors, Queen Victoria honours the City with her presence on the first Lord Mayor's Day after her accession to the Throne, (1837). We see her again, accompanied by her Consort, 'Albert the Good,' in the year of the great Exhibition (1851). Upon this occasion the ancient Crypt of the Guildhall is fitted

up in the style of an old baronial hall, and provided with
suitable furniture. The valuable plate of the City Companies
is displayed upon an oak sideboard. In each of the recesses are
placed mirrors, and from the walls are suspended tapestries copied
from the famous examples at Bayeux, representing the incidents
connected with the conquest of England by William I. Around
the columns supporting the roof, City Policemen stand clad in
suits of armour brought from the Tower—the whole scene is one
of magnificence and splendour. The Crimean war has come to
an end (1856). Our allies in that war, the Emperor of the
French (accompanied by the Empress), and a little later, in
the same year, the King of Sardinia, are entertained with great
splendour. Eight years later, the Prince and Princess of Wales
are entertained with becoming honour and dignity on the
occasion of their marriage. We may see a welcome—such
as the City delights in giving—in 1867, to the ill-fated Abdul
Aziz, Sultan of Turkey ; in 1871, to H.R.H. Prince Arthur ; in
1873, and again in 1889, to the Shah of Persia; in 1875, to
Alexander II., Czar of Russia ; in 1876, to the Prince of Wales
on his return from India ; in 1881, to the King of the Hellenes ;
and in 1886, the year of the Colonial and Indian Exhibition,
the representatives of the different Colonies are received and
welcomed. But brilliant as all these gatherings have been, they
are eclipsed by the preparations for, and the assembly which
met on, the occasion of the celebration of the Queen's Jubilee
in 1887. We see there present, four Kings, the reigning
sovereigns of Denmark, Belgium, Saxony and Greece ; the
Prince and Princess of Wales and nearly every Member of
the Royal Family; representatives of various reigning families
of Europe, including the present Czar of Russia and the present
Emperor of Germany, then joyous young Princes ; the
Ambassadors of Austria, France, Russia, Germany, Turkey,
and Italy ; the Ministers of nearly every State in the World; a
host of the most distinguished men of the time ; and, last but not
least, a number of the Princes of India in their gorgeous attire.

Five thousand guests are present, which taxes to the utmost the accommodation of the Guildhall, and presents a spectacle that no one who witnessed it will ever forget. Since that brilliant gathering, we may recall stately entertainments to do honour to the present German Emperor ; to the great African Explorer, Stanley; to celebrate the Jubilee of the Penny Postage ; and to welcome the International Congress of Hygiene and Demography ; and still fresh in our memory, (1897) the Ball and Reception in honour of the Diamond Jubilee of our honoured and gracious Majesty, Victoria, Queen of Great Britain and Ireland, Empress of India.

Such briefly, are some of the stirring historic scenes, political, social and personal, that this Guildhall of ours, during the centuries of its existence, has witnessed. But there is another aspect of the work there, that must not be forgotten. During these centuries, amidst turmoil and trouble, there passes before our eyes a vision of innumerable applicants for assistance—the widow, the fatherless, the oppressed, the champion and advocate of every cause, that has for its aim the well-being of our fellow-man,—who have all received a welcome there,—and, during the whole of its lengthened and glorious career, its doors have never been shut to such, while the many who entered with sad, but hopeful hearts, have, if their case has been found deserving, never been sent empty away.

In concluding this brief summary of the scenes, upon which imagination may easily, and with profit dwell, we cannot do better than quote the words of prominent public men as to the Guildhall and its work.

Speaking in the Guildhall, the late Rt. Hon. W. E. Gladstone once said :—

" On every great occasion, in every great crisis of the history of the country, when there has, unfortunately, been a conflict among its constitutional powers, it has been commonly found that the side taken by the City of London has likewise been the side adopted by the House of Commons."

On another occasion, the same statesman said :—

"In the Lord Mayor of London, they saw no unfit representative of that Municipal system which was so closely connected with the liberties they so highly prized. Five centuries had passed over the Hall in which they now were gathered, and it was left still as firm and as able to withstand the vicissitudes of the elements as it was on the day it was founded. In the same manner, the Local Institutions of the City, still earlier in their date, yet retained down to this hour a vigorous life. Whenever reformation was applied, it was always applied to them in a spirit of reverence and caution, and they came out from it, as had been seen on a thousand occasions, fresher and stronger than before."

Sir William Harcourt, when Home Secretary, said, "there are no traditions more illustrious than those which cluster around the Guildhall. I should be as averse to destroying the Guildhall, as to destroying Westminster Hall or the Abbey."

A few years later, the Rt. Hon. Joseph Chamberlain said, "its history and great traditions, of which every citizen has a right to be proud, have given to the Corporation of London that affectionate regard that is one of the privileges of age. The Guildhall is intimately associated with the history of the City proper, and is connected with its past struggles, with the glorious fight that has been made for liberty, and with its sturdy resistance even to the oppression of kings."

At a recent Lord Mayor's Banquet, Sir Matthew White Ridley, Home Secretary, said, "the Lord Mayor and Corporation of the City of London have a great and noble tradition—they have a unique record of self-government, which is dear to the hearts and convictions of the English people, and which has taken a splendid place in our national history. They have achieved a prestige up to which it will be difficult to act, but which, I believe, still animates their conduct, and, as to which, it is still thought by the people of this country that they are not acting in a manner unworthy of their great predecessors."

At the same banquet, Lord Salisbury, Prime Minister of England—himself a descendant of more than one of London's Lord Mayors—said, "amid the changes of modern life, the Lord Mayor and the Corporation of London occupy much the position they have occupied for many generations. I hope that these entertainments will be, as they always have been, a sign of the splendid position which the Corporation occupies, not only in English life, but in the eyes of Europe."

A Guide to Guildhall.

The Guildhall.

THE visitor passing along King Street from Cheapside, obtains a strikingly picturesque view of the historic Guildhall of the City of London. On crossing Gresham Street, the Church of St. Lawrence Jewry is seen on the left, a church intimately connected with the City's official life, as the scene of the religious service, held previous to the annual election of the Lord Mayor on Michaelmas Day. It is one of Wren's churches, opened in 1677, built at a cost of over £10,000, and was the most expensive of his City churches. Its predecessor—burnt down in the Great Fire, 1666—had a history of at least 400 years. Beyond this, is a drinking fountain erected in 1866 to commemorate the pious benefactors (from 1375 to 1765) of the Parishes of St. Lawrence Jewry and St. Mary Magdalene. The sculpture on this fountain is the work of Joseph Durham, R.A. Opposite to this on the right, and standing back from the roadway, is the Irish Chamber, built in 1825. Here is transacted the business of the Honourable, the Irish Society, incorporated by Royal Charter in 1613. This Society manages the City's estates in Londonderry and Coleraine, which were allotted to the Corporation on the plantation of Ulster in 1609, a work carried out at the instigation of King James I.

Adjoining, and extending to Basinghall Street, is the City of London Court. The first stone of this building was laid by Lord Chancellor Halsbury in 1887. At the South-east corner of Guildhall Yard, opposite the Irish Chamber, are the offices of the Lord Mayor's Court and the Land Tax Commissioners for the City. These occupy part of the site of the Courts of Queen's Bench and Common Pleas, which were built in 1823 but disused in 1883, when the new Law Courts in the Strand were opened.

As we pass on towards the Guildhall, on the right is the entrance to the Art Gallery, which is open free to the public from 10 a.m. to 5 p.m. (see page 94). On the opposite side of the broad open space known as the Guildhall Yard is the Guildhall Justice Room, where an Alderman sits daily as magistrate. In the upper portion of this building are the offices of the Remembrancer and the City Solicitor. While standing here, the visitor may be interested in watching the pigeons in the Yard. They are regularly fed by the officials, and many have become so tame that they will perch on an outstretched hand, and calmly feed from its palm. Here, also, an exterior survey of the Porch of the Guildhall may be taken. Although its appearance is not so imposing as when originally built (1425-1430) it yet retains much of its old grandeur. The erection above it, dating from 1782 only, with the City Arms, supporting the Cap of Maintenance and the City's Motto, "*Domine Dirige Nos*," and the pile of buildings on the left, reflect but slight credit upon the Clerk of the City's Works at that date. From 1828 until 1873, when the present Library was opened, the rooms over the Porch, and the upper apartments in the East wing of the Front, now removed, were used as a part of the Library, and the former is still an adjunct thereto. The lower portion of the building on the left is used by the Comptroller and his Staff; while the upper rooms serve as a residence for the Keeper of the Guildhall.

Photo by the L. S. & P. Co., Ld.

THE GUILDHALL PORCH.

C

The Porch.

THE entrance to the Hall from Guildhall Yard is through a bold and large Gothic archway on the south side. It forms the principal entrance, and was erected in the years 1425-30. Stow records that the foundation of the Porch " was laide in the fourth year of the raigne of Henry VI." He says,

"Then was builded the Maior's chamber and the counsell chamber, with other rooms above the staires. Last of all, a stately porch entering the Great Hall was erected, the front thereof towards the south being beautified with images of stone."

These 'images of stone,' seven in number, represented Law, Learning, Discipline, Justice, Fortitude, and Temperance, with the figure of our Saviour surmounting the whole. This addition to the Hall was one of the most imposing features of the edifice, and prior to the erection of the structures on each side of it from the designs of Mr. Dance, in the year 1789, was considerably in advance of the main building. Though subjected to minor alterations from time to time, its chief points of interest are uninjured. These combine two bays of groined vaulting, the walls having deeply recessed, moulded, and traceried panelling, varied where the side doorways to the office of the Comptroller of the Chamber and Library corridor occur, and provided with a convenient bench against the side walls. The vaulting is richly groined with moulded principal and secondary ribs, springing from corresponding pillars, the intersections being enriched with handsome sculptured bosses of heraldic and foliated devices in varied designs, emblazoned and gilt, the two principal bosses bearing the Arms of Edward

the Confessor and Henry VI. Among others is the eagle of
St. John, the ox of St. Luke, the lion of St. Mark, the angel
of St. Matthew, and the monogram IHS.

ARMS OF EDWARD THE
CONFESSOR.

ARMS OF HENRY VI.

From the Porch, through a pair of exceedingly handsome
oak doors, we enter the historic Guildhall, in which have been
enacted a greater number of glorious scenes of national importance than in any building in the kingdom, or perhaps in the
whole world; "the place where the citizens have for ages
been accustomed to assemble, not only to transact municipal
business, but also freely to discuss public grievances, to consider
and suggest remedies for great social evils, and to promote the
general interests of humanity." We are at once struck with its
magnificent proportions and general appearance of vastness—a
vastness enhanced by its beautiful open timbered roof.

₮ₕₑ Great Hall.

IT seems desirable, before proceeding to describe the Great Hall, as we see it now, that some account should be given of its erection, and of the buildings that preceded it. Space will not permit of any mention of the various traditions and speculations as to the existence of a Hall as the meeting place of the citizens, and where, in after years, the various Trade Guilds met for the transaction of business, earlier than the reign of Edward the Confessor, A.D. 1041-1066, and that there was one at that time can only be surmised from the fact, that the arms of Edward appear not only in the Porch, but in the Crypt, and other portions of the present Guildhall. This, however, may be very slight proof, but it must be remarked that such a belief evidently existed when the later Hall was built—otherwise the Arms would hardly have been selected as a companion to those of Henry VI., in whose reign the present Hall was completed. Stow asserts that the first Guildhall was situated on the east side of Aldermanbury, and the City Archives seem to favour this view. The present hall is east of Aldermanbury and in close proximity to it.

Early in the 15th century the necessities of the time caused by the improvement of commerce at home, and the increase of trade with foreign countries, led to an enlargement of the Hall, which was found to be inadequate; and in the year 1411 a new building was commenced. This was an event of much moment—Fabyan, the Alderman of Farringdon Ward Without, recording the fact in his Chronicles (1490) in the following quaint manner :—

"1411. In this yere was ye Guyld Halle, of London, began to be new edyfied, and of an oylde and lytell cotage made into a fayre and goodly house as it nowe apperyth."

Stow, in reference to this re-building, remarks—

"That towards the charges thereof the companies gave large benevolences; also offences of men were pardoned for sums of money towards this work, extraordinary fees were raised, fines, amercements, and other things employed during seven years with a continuation thereof three years more, all to be employed to this building."

The term of ten years mentioned seems to have been far exceeded. The necessity for raising the money by means of fines is shown by a reference to the matter in one of the Corporation Letter Books, 14 March, 14 Henry IV., 1412-13 :—

Whereas the new work of the Guildhall, begun and kept up by the pious alms and help of various citizens and others deceased, had ceased, to the manifest scandal and disgrace of the City, it was provided by the Mayor, William Waldern, and the Aldermen, and others of the Common Council assembled, that certain articles should be observed for the next six years. Then follows a list of fines, amercements, and fees. The term during which fines, &c., were to be levied seems to have been far exceeded—for the order seem to have remained in force until the year 1439, when the Hall was nearly completed. In addition to the amount received from fines, &c., the King, Henry V., by allowing "free passage of lime, ragstone, and freestone by land or by water," gave assistance, and various presentations and bequests were made by the citizens for the continuance of the work. For example, we find that in the year 1417 John Wollaston, one of the executors of John Beamond, paid to the new work at Guildhall £60 out of the goods of the testator; in 1422, John Coventry and John Carpenter, executors of Sir Richard Whitington, contributed towards the paving of the great Hall £20, and the next year £15 more "to the said pavement with hard stone of Purbeck"; they also glazed some windows thereof, "on every which window the arms of Richard Whitington are placed." The Hall seems to have been still in some degree unfinished in 1439, for we find the executors of another citizen bringing in £20 "towards the sustentation of the work at the Guildhall." Stow also records that in 1505 Nicholas Alwyn gave by his testament "for a hanging tapestry to serve for principal days in the Guildhall, £73 6s. 8d." The two lanterns, or turrets, which were distinguishing features in the Hall, were not added until 1499. The Hall, thus completed, stood, in all essential respects, until the great fire of 1666, when the open, lofty-pitched oak roof was partly destroyed, and the principal front much injured; its appearance during the fire is thus described by Vincent in "God's Terrible Voice in the City:"

"That night the sight of Guildhall was a fearful spectacle, which stood, the whole body of it together in view, for several hours together after the fire had taken it, without flames (I suppose because the timber was such solid oake), in a bright shining coale as if it had been a pallace of gold, or a great building of burnished brass.'

From other contemporary accounts the roof was evidently found to be so much injured that it was necessary to take it down.

In rebuilding, the walls were considerably heightened. Blome, a diarist (1670-1693), says :—

"The roofs, floor, and what else was therein, were consumed—these rooms, courts, and offices are appropriated to the same place wherein they were kept formerly, but much more regular and loftier, and more substantially built. The great Hall being formerly in height as to the upright of the walls, 30 feet, which are now raised 20 feet higher on either side and at both ends, where there are four windows and eight large windows at either side, each 16 feet high, where there were none before, and over all the flat roof and platform leaded, whereas, before, the roof did meet at the top as in common dwellings."

So it would appear that the old open timber roof gave way to a flat one ; this was attributed to Wren, who is said to have built it in haste for immediate use, and only as a temporary covering. It proved, however, to be more than temporary. It remained for 200 years, when it was replaced (1864) by the present handsome roof, from the design of the late Sir Horace Jones, the City Architect, which has been acknowledged by eminent architects to be consistent in design with the style of architecture in fashion at the period when the Guildhall was extended and enlarged (1411-1439).

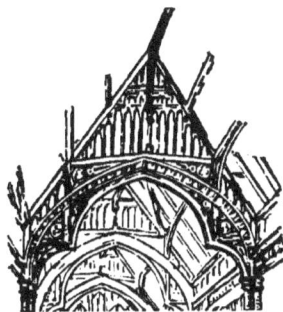

EXISTING ROOF.   ANCIENT ROOF.

The similarity of design between the original and the present roof will at once be seen by referring to the illustrations given above.

The following is an authoritative architectural description of the Great Hall :—

" The Hall is divided into eight bays or divisions on north and south walls by engaged piers, formed by a group of three clustered shafts or pillars, connected vertically by intermediate mouldings, the whole having moulded bases with stilted plinths and surmounted by similar clustered capitals, with sculptured floriated enrichments, all in gilt. These shafted piers rise to the soffit of the main cornice. The wall surfaces on sides and west end under gallery are overlaid with traceried and cusped panelling, generally in two divisions, with certain exceptions as openings, etc., and the west end, comprising arches, mullions, transoms and other sub-divisions and mouldings, with six fine sculptured corbels to three windows on the north wall.

" The lower compartments form a high dado or wall-basement with elevated plinth, and surmounted with a cornice, enriched by an interesting series of City shields, heads, animals, and other pateræ, and crowned by an embattled cresting. In connection with this basement, a bench, or stone seat, cased with oak, is introduced. The whole is surmounted (on the sides) by a fine string-course and frieze, crowned with a cornice containing heraldic and other varied pateræ enrichments, emblazoned and gilt, above which are bold battlements and plain faces which complete the wall surface. This arrangement is cut up into divisions by the roof ribs set upon the capitals, which are level with the bottom of the cornice. The frieze contains a series of mottoes, heraldic supporters, and Shields of Arms relating to England, the Corporation of London, and the twelve principal Livery Companies. The mottoes are in raised Gothic letters of a bold character ; the shields centred between the letters in each bay are emblazoned, and the supporters, or other emblems, at each end of the mottoes, are also decorated, and the lettering gilt, with a background in vermilion. The whole forms a characteristic and appropriate band on each side.

The alterations in connection with the new cornice and other improvements in the restoration of the roof were commenced in the month of May, 1864, in the mayoralty of the Right Honourable William Lawrence, the first stone of the cornice being laid by the chairman of the City Lands Committee on the 22nd June in that year.

" On both sides of these panelled walls are sixteen two-light deeply recessed windows, having acute-pointed arched heads.

filled with cusped tracery, each light divided by a transom. The lower divisions also have traceried and cusped heads. Four of these openings are of less height where the doorways and canopied cornice occur. Immediately under the great east window is a rich arched canopy of stone, with cinque-foiled cuspings foliated, and enclosed in square headed sunk spandrels; over which, completing the exterior, is a cornice with a series of pateræ, and finished with an embattled parapet. This work is returned one bay on each side, thereby defining the dais, and is elevated seven feet higher than the adjacent basement. At the two opposite angles a corbelling is placed to receive the groups of columns from which spring the outer arches of the great window, and the centre is further enriched by a similar projection. A beautiful and delicate work of arcading with columns and vaulting arches with cinque-foiled cuspings, foliated, and a profusion of carved bossings, enrich the recessed surfaces, etc., sunk behind this overhanging tabernacled cornice, partially obscured for want of decorative assistance to lighten up the shadows. At the western end there is a simple moulded cornice across the Hall and running beneath the window.

"At each end of the Hall, occupying the entire width, is a magnificent window ; both are similar as regards design generally, but somewhat varied in details. They are filled with stained glass, which produces rich and decorative effect, but is so toned that the admission of light is not sensibly obscured, but only softened. The great hood-mouldings spring from the caps of clustered pillars : at the eastern end these are dwarf, the bases being set upon the cornice, but at the western end they rise from the pavement similar to the other pillars of the Hall. There are in each window, two massive mullions of the whole height from sill to archivolt, separating the centre from the side lights, with additional mouldings connected with them on each side. The principal mouldings of these mullions and jambs are finished on to the sill with bases. The centre is divided into five lights by minor mullions, and into two tiers vertically by transoms, and the side lights are double. The heads are richly filled with arches and cusped tracery, and the sub-divisions are similarly treated. Each window has a Shield of the Arms of Edward the Confessor placed in the apex of the arch mouldings. On the tracery of the east windows, right and left in the angles next the mullions, are two shields charged with heraldic devices. On the west window are also two escutcheons, bearing the Arms of the Plantagenet and Lancastrian kings. That on the right hand (Plantagenet) *gu.* three lions *passant guardant* in pale *or*; on the left (Lancastrian) 1st and 4th semé of fleurs-de-lis over their azure field (France), 2nd and 3rd *gu.* three lions *passant guardant* in pale *or.* Over these windows in the gables are openings for the further lighting of the upper space. On each side of the east window, occupying and decorating the space between the shafts and the window jambs, is a small and interesting canopied niche or tabernacle of somewhat like character in its details to the cornice. It contains a sunk three-panelled pedestal with moulded plinth and capping for a statue, and is covered with a three-sided moulded canopy with tre-foiled cusped tracery, which is completed with a tre-foiled cresting; especially noticeable on account of its peculiar finials and foreign treatment.

" The east end of the Hall is fitted with a raised dais or platform. This is ascended by three steps. It is appropriated for holding the Court of Husting. Here also sit (on a raised platform placed on the dais) the Lord Mayor, Aldermen, Sheriffs, Chief Officers, and many of the prominent members of the Livery at the meetings of the Common Hall for the election of Lord Mayor, Sheriffs, Chamberlain, etc., and other public meetings called by the Lord Mayor. The wall at back and one bay on each side, are lined with very rich and elaborate oak panelling, finished with a coved and groined canopy, all enriched with moulded and carved work. Three canopied niches with pedestals for statues are introduced, in position corresponding with the corbellings of the stone cornice. A doorway in the south bay, concealed in the panelling, gives access to a vestibule in connection with the Library buildings, and, also, to the corridor attached to the porch at Guildhall Yard. Another similar opening (north) connects the hall with the new Council Chamber, when such may be required on important occasions. In the south bay close to the Porch doors, is an Oak Screen and Buffet which is divided into three bays, decorated with Gothic panels and furnished with shelves for the exhibition of the Corporation plate—the middle upper panel is provided with brackets for supporting the sword and mace when the Lord Mayor takes his seat at a State Banquet—the Arms are those of Sir David Evans and Sir Stuart Knill, Lord Mayors, and Sir George Tyler, Sir Joseph Renals, Sir Walter Wilkin, and Mr. H. S. Foster, Sheriffs, in whose respective terms of office .the work was carried out. The Arms of Mr. W. H. Pannell and Mr. G. N. Johnson, "Chief Commoners" during the execution of the work, also appear. At the west end, through the two openings in the screen, access is provided to the Law Courts and other chambers, etc., and by stairs to the gallery turrets, and also to the Crypt. The small centre doorway is reputed to be ancient.

"The floor is paved principally with Portland stone, arranged in panels of large dimensions. These are divided by bands of tiles, and the whole connected by borders of black and buff tiles, and completed outside with similar white stone pavements. These panels are enriched with incised quatrefoils and ornamental figures. In the panels down the centre of the pavement, commencing from the East End, are first, the Arms of Henry VI., in whose reign the Guildhall was built, and then alternately the Arms of the City of London and the Royal Arms."

In the stone panels down the sides of the floor of the Hall are the Arms (filled in with lead) of the following Mayors :—

NORTH SIDE.		SOUTH SIDE.	
HENRY FITZ-EYLWIN	.. 1189-1213	SIR WM. WALWORTH..	1374, 80
SIR RD. WHITINGTON	1396, 97, 1406, 19	SIR THOMAS KNOLLES	1399, 1411
SIR RICHARD GRESHAM	 1537	SIR THOMAS WHITE..	.. 1553
SIR EDWARD OSBORNE	 1583	SIR THOMAS MYDDELTON..	1613
SIR HENRY TULSE	 1684	SIR RICHARD HOARE..	.. 1713
WILLIAM BECKFORD, ESQ.	 1763	SIR THOMAS GABRIEL	.. 1867

The official standard of length may be observed marked on brass plates across the floor. On the North wall at the West end of the Hall is a tablet containing the following inscription :—

STANDARDS OF LENGTH
(AT 62° FAHRENHEIT)
PLACED IN THIS HALL
BY THE CORPORATION OF THE
CITY OF LONDON,
1878.

THE STANDARD OF LENGTHS OF
100 FEET AND 66 FEET
ARE LAID DOWN ON THE FLOOR
IN FRONT OF THIS TABLET.

STANDARDS OF LENGTH.
ONE FOOT. TWO FEET. IMPERIAL YARD.

These standards were laid under the superintendence of the late Sir George Airy, Astronomer Royal, and certified by the Board of Trade.

Brass ornamental perforated gratings are inserted for the introduction of heated air into the building. Coronæ suspended from the roof in the bays between the principals provide for the artificial illumination of the Hall. The electric light was installed both here and throughout the Guildhall buildings in 1889. A powerful sun-burner is fixed in 'the lantern' of the fleche, for illumination and ventilation.

"The size of the Large Hall will be better understood by comparison with similar large buildings, both ancient and modern, existing here and on the Continent. One of the earliest of which we have any accurate measurement is probably that in the Baths of Diocletian at Rome, now the Church of S. Maria degli Angeli ; this is upwards of 300 feet in length."

	LENGTH.	WIDTH.	HEIGHT.
	FT.	FT.	FT.
Hall in the Baths of Diocletian, now the Church of S. Maria degli Angeli, Rome	308	74	84
Basilica, remains of Roman City at Silchester	268	60	—
Westminster Hall..	238	67½	90
Palazzo della Ragione, Padua ..	261	88	80
Christ's Hospital, London	187	51	47
Palazzo Vecchio, Florence	184	73	70
Hatfield Hall, Durham ..	180	50	—
St. George's Hall, Liverpool	170	74	83
Palazzo del Podesta, Bologna ..	170	46	—
Palazzo della Ragione, Vicenza	169	69	—
GUILDHALL, LONDON	152	49½	89
Town Hall, Birmingham	140	65	65

Stained Glass Windows.

Eastern Window.

THE handsome Memorial Window at the eastern end of the Hall was presented to the Corporation by the Operatives of Lancashire and the Cotton Districts on the 15th July, 1870, in acknowledgment of assistance during the Cotton Famine (1862-65).

The middle division in both tiers is devoted to representations of historical subjects connected with the history of the City of London. The couplet division on the north side contains figures of Lancashire worthies. In the similar division on the south side are introduced worthies of the City. The subject of the lower tier of the central portion of the window is illustrative of the rebuilding of the City by Alfred the Great, that of the upper tier being devoted to the subject of the grant of the Charter to the City of London by William I. In the side division on the north side are full length portraits of Sir Richard Whitington and Sir Thomas Gresham ; on the south, John of Gaunt, Duke of Lancaster, and Sir Thomas Stanley. The heraldic bearings proper to each are introduced in the traceried openings above. In the tracery of the main portion of the window are represented the shields of the twelve great livery companies (the Mercers, Grocers, Drapers, Fishmongers, Goldsmiths, Skinners, Merchant Taylors, Haberdashers, Salters, Ironmongers, Vintners and Clothworkers).

At the base of the window is the following inscription :—

The Grateful Memorial of the Operatives of Lancashire and the Cotton Manufacturing Districts to the Mansion House Relief Committee, who, as almoners of a world's benevolence, distributed to them more than £500,000 during the Cotton Famine, 1862-65, namely, William Cubitt, Lord Mayor ; William James Richmond Cotton, Charles Barber, William Morley, John Armitage, Groom Howes, Francis Lycett, and Stauros Dilberoglue ; with Lord Mayors William Anderson Rose, William Lawrence, Warren Stormes Hale ; and Joseph Gibbs, Secretary.

FIRST WINDOW ON SOUTH SIDE FROM EAST END.

The subject represented is the Restoration of the City Charter in 1688 ; in one light of the window are portrayed the Lord Mayor, Sword and Mace Bearers, and a Man-at-Arms ; in the other light, the Lord Chancellor, Purse Bearer, Courtiers, and a Man-at-Arms. In the tracery are the armorial bearings of the late Mr. Deputy Harris, and of the Saddlers' Company.

Presented to the Corporation of London by Henry Harris, Esq., Deputy for the Ward of Lime Street, and Master of the Saddlers' Company, 1874.

SECOND WINDOW ON SOUTH SIDE FROM EAST END.

The two upper lights represent King Edward VI. passing to Westminster to be crowned, 19th February, 1547. The spectators are the Master and the Liverymen of the Saddlers' Company in their gowns, and the Officers of the Court of the Guild. The horse, the cognizance of the Company, is a conspicuous feature. The two lower lights represent the Reception by Sir Henry Picard, Lord Mayor of London, 1363, of Five Kings on their landing at Queenhithe, viz. :—Edward III. of England, David of Scotland, John of France, Magnus II. of Denmark, and the King of Cyprus. The arms of the Saddlers' Company and of the Donor appear in the tracery above the upper portion of the window.

Presented by Archibald MacDougall, Esq., Deputy, 1874.

WINDOW OVER ALDERMAN BECKFORD'S MONUMENT.

The upper lights of this window contain the story of Rahere's Dream, and the Vision to him of St. Bartholomew ; the lower lights have for their subject the Founding by Rahere of the Hospital and Church of St. Bartholomew the Great, in Smithfield, A.D. 1102. In the tracery are figures of angels bearing shields with the Arms of Alderman Farncomb, Lord Mayor, 1849, and Alderman Stone, Lord Mayor, 1874, and at the base is the following inscription :—

Presented on behalf of the Ward of Bassishaw, by David Henry Stone, Esq., Alderman of that Ward, 1866.

NEXT WINDOW TOWARDS WEST.

The upper lights of this window illustrate the death of Wat Tyler, and the lower ones the knighting by Richard II. of William Walworth, Mayor, a former Prime Warden of the Fishmongers' Company.

Presented by the Fishmongers' Company, 1868.

WINDOW OVER ENTRANCE DOOR.

The left-hand light of this window contains a figure of Sir John Crosby ; the right-hand light, one of Sir John Cutler.

Presented by the Grocers' Company, 1868.

NEXT WINDOW ON SOUTH SIDE.

This window commemorates the visit of the Prince and Princess of Wales to the City upon the return of His Royal Highness from India, 1876. The two upper lights of the window shew the Prince and Princess of Wales being received by Lord Mayor Cotton. The lower two lights—The Princess of Wales partaking of the Loving Cup with the Lord Mayor.

Presented by W. J. R. Cotton, Esq., Alderman of Lime Street Ward, Lord Mayor, 1875, and M.P. for the City of London, 1877.

WINDOW SECOND FROM WEST END.

The subject on the left-hand represents the Jews being banished from this country by Edward I. On the right-hand is shown the Jews petitioning Cromwell, in 1656, to be allowed to again reside here. The lower compartments represent the swearing-in of David Salomons, Esq., as Lord Mayor of London, 1855.

Presented in 1870 by Sir David Salomons, Bart., Citizen and Cooper, Alderman of the Ward of Cordwainer, and M.P. for Greenwich, first of the Jewish Faith chosen Sheriff, 1835; Alderman, 1847; Lord Mayor of this City, 1855; gratefully to acknowledge the impulse given to the cause of religious liberty by the Corporation of London, also to commemorate the removal by Parliament of all obstacles to persons professing the Jewish religion holding public offices.

WINDOW IN SOUTH-WEST ANGLE.

The upper light on the left-hand has the armorial bearings of the City of London, that on the right those of Sir Moses Montefiore ; in the lower left-hand light is a shield with the arms of the County of Kent ; and in the right hand lower light a shield upon which are a harp and crown, symbolical of the East, both shields being surrounded by wreaths of olive and palm leaves.

Presented in 1870 by Sir Moses Montefiore, Bart., Sheriff 1837. High Sheriff of the County of Kent, 1845.

WESTERN WINDOW.

The window at the West End of the Hall has been filled with stained glass by the Corporation, in memory of His Royal Highness the late Prince Consort, and was unveiled by His Royal Highness Prince Arthur on 3rd November, 1870.

D

The leading ideas and occupations of this country, on which the Prince brought to bear so much influence, and which derived such great advantages from his personal encouragement, were chosen as the subjects portrayed in this memorial.

The window is a five-light transomed one. The two side wings are occupied by four figures representing Wisdom, Prudence, Justice, and Fortitude. The lower tier is occupied by the following subjects :—Agriculture, Industry, Trade, Education, Charity, and Commerce.

The upper row contains representations of Music, Poetry, and History ; Peace, Purity, Religion, and Home Prosperity ; Architecture, Painting, and Sculpture ; Science and Literature. In the centre of these is a figure of the Prince, seated in an attitude of meditation, book in hand ; in the back ground are two figures unveiling the Great Exhibition of 1851, an event which exercised much influence on arts and commerce. The smaller upper openings of tracery contain the Royal Arms and those of the City of London, with the personal crests of the Prince, and the several Orders of the Bath, Garter, St. Patrick, St. Michael and St. George, together with the Arms of the City Companies of which the Prince was a member. This window is a fine example of its kind, it has been appropriately described as Mosaic, inasmuch as there are as many as 580 pieces of glass in one square of 30 superficial feet.

WINDOW AT NORTH-WEST CORNER.

1. William the Conqueror holding in his hand the first Charter granted to the City of London.

2. Henry I. presenting the Charter granting to the City of London, the County of Middlesex with London, and the right of Hunting in the Forests.

3. Richard I. granting the Charter conveying to the City of London the Conservancy of the River Thames.

4. Edward VI. presenting the Charter of the Four Royal Hospitals.

Presented by Cornelius Lea Wilson, Esq., 1867.

NEXT WINDOW TOWARDS EAST.

1. Trinobantes : British Inhabitants of London, with a representation of the Tower of London, which was "begun to be builded at the end of the 11th century."

2. The erection of the Roman Wall of London, beneath which is a view of Baynard's Castle.

3. Edward the Confessor recognising the privileges of the Citizens of London : below this is a view of Old London Bridge, which was " begun to be builded in 1176."

4. Edward IV. making four Citizens of London Knights of the Bath. Beneath is a representation of St. John's Gate, Clerkenwell.

This window was presented in 1866, by Samuel Wilson, Esq., Alderman of the Ward of Bridge Without ; Alderman of the Ward of Castle Baynard from 1831 to 1853; Sheriff, 1833 ; Lord Mayor, 1838.

WINDOW OVER THE MONUMENT TO LORD NELSON.

1.—Fitzwalter doing service as Bannerer, 1303.

2.—The youth swearing fealty at Paul's Cross, 1259.

3.—Henry Picard, Mayor, feasting Five Kings, 1363

4.—Holding a great joust on London Bridge, 1395

5.—Edward III. first ordering gold to be coined in the Tower, 1344.

6.—Guildhall building—Thomas Knolles, Mayor 1411.

7.—William Walworth, Mayor, slaying Wat Tyler, 1381.

8.—Henry V. making his triumphal entry into London after Agincourt, 1415.

Put in at the expense of the Corporation, 1866.

WINDOW OVER DOOR LEADING TO COUNCIL CHAMBER LOBBY.

It has, in one compartment, a full-length representation of FitzEylwin, the first Mayor of London, A.D. 1189 to 1213; in the light above is his Coat of Arms; in the lower light are the Arms of the Weavers' Company, with the City Sword, Mace, and Cap of Maintenance arranged beneath. In the other compartment is a similar representation of Whitington, four times Mayor of London, A.D. 1396, 1397, 1406, 1419; in the light above is his Coat of Arms; in the lower light are the City Arms, with the Sceptre, Collar of SS. and Jewel, and the Mayoralty Seal arranged beneath.

Presented by the Weavers' Company, the most ancient of the City Guilds. Samuel Wilson, Esq., Alderman, Upper Bailiff, 1868.

WINDOW OVER MONUMENT TO THE DUKE OF WELLINGTON.

This window contains figures of SS. Andrew, Bride, Helen, and Dunstan, placed under canopies of the Cinque Cento period; one of the churches dedicated in the name of each Saint being introduced in the background, except in the case of S. Helen, where S. Sepulchre, Snow Hill, has been chosen, as she founded the Church of the Holy Sepulchre, at Jerusalem, and as there is no church dedicated to her in Farringdon Without Ward. Beneath the figures are medallions containing views respectively of Holborn Viaduct, Blackfriars Bridge, the New Meat Market in Smithfield, and Temple Bar.

Presented by the Ward of Farringdon Without, 1870.

THIRD WINDOW FROM EASTERN END ON NORTH SIDE.

This represents, in the lowest compartments, the Arms of the Haberdashers' Company, and the Arms of England in the reign of Queen Elizabeth, by whom its Charter was granted. In the upper part are figures of SS. Nicholas and Catherine, the Patron Saints of the Company.

Presented by the Haberdashers' Company, 1867.

WINDOW IN NORTH-WEST ANGLE.

This represents, in the westernmost division, Queen Elizabeth receiving a Hunting Party at "Queen Elizabeth's Lodge," in Epping Forest, and in the other, or easternmost division, Her Most Gracious Majesty, Queen Victoria, receiving an address from the Corporation at High Beech, on the 6th May, 1882, when she expressed her great satisfaction in dedicating the Forest to the enjoyment of her people for ever.

Presented in 1884 by John Thomas Bedford, Esq., a Member of the Corporation, as a Memorial of freeing the Forest.

The Monuments.

THE first Monument on the South side of the Hall is one erected in honour of Lord Mayor Beckford.

BECKFORD'S MONUMENT.

The Monument bears the following inscription :—

SPEECH TO HIS MAJESTY KING GEORGE III.

ON THE 23RD OF MAY 1770.

MOST GRACIOUS SOVEREIGN,

WILL YOUR MAJESTY BE PLEASED SO FAR TO CONDESCEND AS TO PERMIT THE MAYOR OF YOUR LOYAL CITY OF LONDON TO DECLARE, IN YOUR ROYAL PRESENCE, ON BEHALF OF HIS FELLOW CITIZENS, HOW MUCH THE BARE APPREHENSION OF YOUR MAJESTY'S DISPLEASURE WOULD, AT ALL TIMES AFFECT THEIR MINDS; THE DECLARATION OF THAT DISPLEASURE HAS ALREADY FILLED THEM WITH INEXPRESSIBLE ANXIETY, AND WITH THE DEEPEST AFFLICTION. PERMIT ME, SIRE, TO ASSURE YOUR MAJESTY, THAT YOUR MAJESTY HAS NOT IN ALL YOUR DOMINIONS ANY SUBJECTS MORE FAITHFUL, MORE DUTIFUL OR MORE AFFECTIONATE TO YOUR MAJESTY'S PERSON AND FAMILY, OR MORE READY TO SACRIFICE THEIR LIVES AND FORTUNES IN THE MAINTENANCE OF THE TRUE HONOUR AND DIGNITY OF YOUR CROWN.

WE DO THEREFORE, WITH THE GREATEST HUMILITY AND SUBMISSION, MOST EARNESTLY SUPPLICATE YOUR MAJESTY, THAT YOU WILL NOT DISMISS US FROM YOUR PRESENCE, WITHOUT EXPRESSING A MORE FAVOURABLE OPINION OF YOUR FAITHFUL CITIZENS, AND WITHOUT SOME COMFORT, WITHOUT SOME PROSPECT AT LEAST OF REDRESS.

PERMIT ME, SIRE, FARTHER TO OBSERVE, THAT WHOSOEVER HAS ALREADY DARED, OR SHALL HEREAFTER ENDEAVOUR, BY FALSE INSINUATIONS AND SUGGESTIONS, TO ALIENATE YOUR MAJESTY'S AFFECTIONS FROM YOUR LOYAL SUBJECTS IN GENERAL, AND FROM THE CITY OF LONDON IN PARTICULAR, AND TO WITHDRAW YOUR CONFIDENCE IN, AND REGARD FOR YOUR PEOPLE IS AN ENEMY TO YOUR MAJESTY'S PERSON AND FAMILY, A VIOLATOR OF THE PUBLIC PEACE, AND A BETRAYER OF OUR HAPPY CONSTITUTION, AS IT WAS ESTABLISHED AT THE GLORIOUS REVOLUTION.

Lord Mayor Beckford is represented in the attitude of addressing this remonstrance to the King, on his Majesty's returning a curt and unfavourable reply to an address from the Corporation formally presented to him on the throne by the Lord Mayor, &c. On one side of this figure is represented the City of London in mourning, and on the other Trade and Navigation in a drooping condition.

Lord Mayor Beckford had served the office of Mayor in 1762, and, although of a great age and in an infirm state of health, and against his wish, was again elected in 1769. He died suddenly on June 21st, 1770. The Monument and Inscription were voted by the Common Council on the 5th July, following, and were unveiled 11th May, 1772. It is the work of a Mr. Moore, and cost the Corporation £1,300.

———————————

On the north side in the second bay or division is placed a Monument to commemorate the celebrated

WILLIAM PITT, EARL OF CHATHAM.

This minister, statesman, and orator, is represented by the artist with all his characteristic sternness. He is attired in classic costume, standing upon a rock, with his left hand on the rudder or helm of State, and his right reclining on an allegorical figure of Commerce, introduced by the City of London, represented by a mural-crowned female figure. Britannia is seen reposing upon a lion, and infantile figures, emblematical of the four quarters of the globe, are pouring forth into her lap treasures from the Cornucopia of Plenty. Figures of anchors, sails and masts with ropes and other details connected with navigation and industry, make up the background of the composition. On the pedestal is a Cap of Liberty, on the headband of which is the word *Libertas*.

The group is from the hands of John Bacon, R.A., (1782), and the cost to the Corporation of the memorial was no less than £3,421 4s. od. This amount included the preparation of the inscription, pedestal, &c. The inscription,

as follows, is said to have been composed by the celebrated
Edmund Burke :—

IN GRATEFUL ACKNOWLEDGEMENT TO THE SUPREME DISPOSER OF EVENTS,
WHO INTENDING TO ADVANCE THIS NATION,
FOR SUCH TIME AS TO HIS WISDOM SEEMED GOOD, TO AN HIGH PITCH OF
PROSPERITY AND GLORY ; BY UNANIMITY AT HOME ;
BY CONFIDENCE AND REPUTATION ABROAD ;
BY ALLIANCES WISELY CHOSEN AND FAITHFULLY OBSERVED ; BY COLONIES
UNITED AND PROTECTED ; BY DECISIVE VICTORIES BY SEA AND LAND ;
BY CONQUESTS MADE BY ARMS AND GENEROSITY IN EVERY PART OF THE GLOBE ;
BY COMMERCE, FOR THE FIRST TIME UNITED WITH,
AND MADE TO FLOURISH BY WAR ; WAS
PLEASED TO RAISE UP AS A PRINCIPAL INSTRUMENT IN THIS MEMORABLE WORK,

WILLIAM PITT.

THE MAYOR, ALDERMEN, AND COMMON COUNCIL,
MINDFUL OF THE BENEFITS WHICH THE CITY OF LONDON RECEIVED IN HER
AMPLE SHARE IN THE GENERAL PROSPERITY,
HAVE ERECTED TO THE MEMORY OF THIS EMINENT STATESMAN AND
POWERFUL ORATOR, THIS MONUMENT IN HER GUILDHALL ; THAT HER CITIZENS
MAY NEVER MEET FOR THE TRANSACTION OF THEIR AFFAIRS
WITHOUT BEING REMINDED THAT THE MEANS BY WHICH PROVIDENCE RAISES A
NATION TO GREATNESS ARE THE VIRTUES INFUSED INTO GREAT MEN ;
AND THAT TO WITHHOLD FROM THOSE VIRTUES,
EITHER OF THE LIVING OR THE DEAD, THE TRIBUTE OF ESTEEM AND
VENERATION, IS TO DENY TO THEMSELVES THE MEANS
OF HAPPINESS AND HONOUR.
THIS DISTINGUISHED PERSON, FOR THE SERVICES RENDERED TO KING
GEORGE THE SECOND AND TO KING GEORGE THE THIRD,
WAS CREATED

EARL OF CHATHAM.

THE BRITISH NATION HONOURED HIS MEMORY WITH A PUBLIC FUNERAL
AND A PUBLIC MONUMENT AMONGST HER ILLUSTRIOUS MEN
IN WESTMINSTER ABBEY.

In the fourth compartment, on the north side, is placed
the Monument erected by the Corporation to the memory of

Arthur Wellesley, Duke of Wellington.

It is well known that the illustrious general passed half his life in peace and half in war. In the Memorial at Guildhall this view is taken for illustration. Peace, seated at the Duke's right hand, extends a civic wreath, and looks up gratefully towards him ; War, seated at his left, leaning on his sheathed sword, and grasping a victor's wreath, rests from his labours. The Duke, erect between the two, rests his left hand on his field marshal's baton, and his right holds the Peace of 1815 ; his regard is towards Peace. He is represented in his usual costume, with the addition of the Ribbon of the Garter, the Star of the Bath, the Waterloo Medal, and a military cloak. The age chosen for the statue is between fifty and sixty, the Duke having then, after the termination of his active military career, passed some years in the acts of peace. Each of these three figures is 8 feet 6 inches in stature. The division of subject is continued ornamentally below. Beneath the figure of War is a shield, with the crest and armorial motto of the Duke ; viz., the lion's head and *Virtutis fortuna comes.* Beneath the figure of Peace is a similar shield, with a dove bearing an olive branch, and the motto (from the Æneid) *Pacis imponere morem,* indicating the Duke's powers of negotiation and administration. Between these shields, in front, is represented in relievo, the last charge at Waterloo (this action dividing a long war from a European Peace of thirty-eight years). On the upper pedestal wreathed with laurel, appear the words WISDOM, DUTY, HONOUR ; on the summit of the entablature appears the name of the hero and the words, born 1769, died 1852. The whole Monument pairs well with that of Nelson, to which it is appendant in situation, and in some degree in treatment. The figures, shields, and relievo are in Carrara marble, as is also the masonry of the Monument itself. This Memorial to the Duke was executed in 1857 by John Bell, R.A., at an expense to the Corporation of £4,966 10s.

Photo. by the L. S. & P. Co., Ld.

WELLINGTON'S MONUMENT.

In the sixth division of the Hall, and upon the same side is a Monument in commemoration of

ADMIRAL LORD NELSON.

The pyramid, on the background, is supposed to be the tomb of

Photo. by the L. S. & P. Co., Ld.

NELSON'S MONUMENT.

the immortal hero decorated with naval trophies, the fruit of his
victories ; while the female figure in the centre (personating the
City of London), in grateful remembrance of the signal services
he rendered to this country, perpetuates the memory of his

great actions to posterity, and finishes with admiration the record of his last glorious achievement of Trafalgar. Britannia, on the left, supported by a Lion (the symbol of unshaken courage) is pensively musing over the portrait of the conqueror, and in silent grief deplores her loss. The recumbent figure in the foreground, representing Neptune, roused by the fame of his heroic actions, participates in Britannia's sorrow and regret for her hero's fate. The naval action in front of the pedestal, exhibits the situation of the fleet towards the close of the battle, when Nelson was mortally wounded by a shot from the main-top of a French seventy-four, with which ship the Victory appears to be closely engaged. In the niches, two British seamen, with implements of war and navigation, hear with deep concern of the fate of their beloved com-mander. The Memorial, the work of the sculptor, James Smith, was executed for the Corporation in 1810, at an expense of £4,442 7s. 4d.

The inscription was written by Rd. Brinsley Sheridan :—

TO HORATIO, VISCOUNT AND BARON NELSON,

VICE-ADMIRAL OF THE WHITE,

AND KNIGHT OF THE MOST HONOURABLE ORDER OF THE BATH.

A MAN AMONGST THE FEW, WHO APPEAR AT DIFFERENT PERIODS TO HAVE
BEEN CREATED TO PROMOTE THE GRANDEUR, AND ADD TO THE
SECURITY OF NATIONS, INCITING BY THEIR HIGH EXAMPLE
THEIR FELLOW MORTALS, THROUGH ALL SUCCEEDING TIMES, TO PURSUE
THE COURSE THAT LEADS TO THE EXALTATION OF OUR
IMPERFECT NATURE.

PROVIDENCE, THAT IMPLANTED IN NELSON'S BREAST AN ARDENT PASSION
FOR DESERVED RENOWN, AS BOUNTEOUSLY ENDOWED HIM WITH
THE TRANSCENDENT TALENTS NECESSARY TO THE GREAT
PURPOSES HE WAS DESTINED TO ACCOMPLISH.
AT AN EARLY PERIOD OF LIFE HE ENTERED INTO THE NAVAL SERVICE OF
HIS COUNTRY; AND EARLY WERE THE INSTANCES WHICH MARKED THE
FEARLESS NATURE AND DARING ENTERPRISE OF HIS CHARACTER;

UNITING TO THE LOFTIEST SPIRIT, AND THE JUSTEST TITLE
TO SELF-CONFIDENCE, A STRICT AND HUMBLE OBEDIENCE TO THE
SOVEREIGN RULE OF DISCIPLINE AND SUBORDINATION,
RISING BY DUE GRADATION TO COMMAND, HE INFUSED INTO THE BOSOMS
OF THOSE HE LED THE VALOROUS ARDOUR AND ENTHUSIASTIC ZEAL FOR
THE SERVICE OF HIS KING AND COUNTRY, WHICH ANIMATED HIS OWN;
AND WHILE HE ACQUIRED THE LOVE OF ALL BY THE SWEETNESS
AND MODERATION OF HIS TEMPER, HE INSPIRED A UNIVERSAL CONFIDENCE
IN THE NEVER-FAILING RESOURCES OF HIS CAPACIOUS MIND.

IT WILL BE FOR HISTORY TO RELATE THE MANY GREAT EXPLOITS, THROUGH
WHICH, SOLICITOUS OF PERIL AND REGARDLESS OF WOUNDS,
HE BECAME THE GLORY OF HIS PROFESSION;
BUT IT BELONGS TO THIS BRIEF RECORD OF HIS ILLUSTRIOUS CAREER
TO SAY, THAT HE COMMANDED AND CONQUERED AT THE
BATTLES OF THE NILE AND COPENHAGEN;
VICTORIES NEVER BEFORE EQUALLED, YET AFTERWARDS SURPASSED BY HIS
OWN LAST ACHIEVEMENT, THE BATTLE OF TRAFALGAR, FOUGHT ON
THE 21ST OF OCTOBER, IN THE YEAR 1805.

ON THAT DAY, BEFORE THE CONCLUSION OF THE ACTION,
HE FELL MORTALLY WOUNDED;
BUT THE SOURCES OF LIFE AND SENSE FAILED NOT, UNTIL IT WAS
KNOWN TO HIM, THAT, THE DESTRUCTION OF THE ENEMY BEING COMPLETED,
THE GLORY OF HIS COUNTRY AND HIS OWN,
HAD ATTAINED THEIR SUMMIT;
THEN, LAYING HIS HAND ON HIS BRAVE HEART, WITH A LOOK OF
EXALTED RESIGNATION TO THE WILL OF THE SUPREME
DISPOSER OF THE FATE OF MAN AND NATIONS, HE EXPIRED.

THE LORD MAYOR, ALDERMEN, AND COMMON COUNCIL OF THE CITY OF
LONDON HAVE CAUSED THIS MONUMENT TO BE ERECTED;
NOT IN THE PRESUMPTUOUS HOPE OF SUSTAINING
THE DEPARTED HERO'S MEMORY,
BUT TO MANIFEST THEIR ESTIMATION OF THE MAN, AND THEIR
ADMIRATION OF HIS DEEDS.
THIS TESTIMONY OF THEIR GRATITUDE, THEY TRUST, WILL REMAIN AS
LONG AS THEIR OWN RENOWNED CITY SHALL EXIST.
THE PERIOD TO NELSON'S FAME CAN ONLY BE THE END OF TIME.

Upon the south side of the Hall, and in the second compartment, is erected the Memorial to the

RIGHT HON. WILLIAM PITT, SON OF THE EARL OF CHATHAM.

The massy substance on which the figures in this composition, are placed is intended to represent the Island of Great Britain and the surrounding waves. On an elevation in the centre, Pitt appears in his robes as Chancellor of the Exchequer. Below him, on an intermediate foreground, two statues characterise his abilities—Apollo on his right, impersonating Eloquence and Learning ; Mercury on his left, as the representative of Commerce and the Patron of policy. The lower part of the Monument is occupied by a figure of Britannia seated triumphantly on a sea-horse, in her left hand is the usual emblem of Naval power, and her right grasps a thunderbolt. The Memorial was executed for the Corporation by J. G. Bubb, in 1813, at an expense of £4,078 17s. 3d.

The inscription was written by George Canning :—

WILLIAM PITT,

SON OF WILLIAM PITT, EARL OF CHATHAM,

INHERITING THE GENIUS, AND FORMED BY THE PRECEPTS OF HIS FATHER,.

DEVOTED HIMSELF FROM HIS EARLY YEARS TO THE SERVICE OF THE STATE.

CALLED TO THE CHIEF CONDUCT OF THE ADMINISTRATION AFTER THE

CLOSE OF A DISASTROUS WAR,

HE REPAIRED THE EXHAUSTED REVENUES, HE REVIVED AND INVIGORATED·

THE COMMERCE AND PROSPERITY OF THE COUNTRY ;

AND HE HAD RE-ESTABLISHED THE PUBLICK CREDIT ON DEEP AND

SURE FOUNDATIONS ;

WHEN A NEW WAR WAS KINDLED IN EUROPE, MORE FORMIDABLE THAN ANY·

PRECEDING WAR FROM THE PECULIAR CHARACTER OF ITS DANGERS.

TO RESIST THE ARMS OF FRANCE, WHICH WERE DIRECTED AGAINST THE

INDEPENDENCE OF EVERY GOVERNMENT AND PEOPLE,

TO ANIMATE OTHER NATIONS BY THE EXAMPLE OF GREAT BRITAIN,

TO CHECK THE CONTAGION OF OPINIONS WHICH TENDED TO DISSOLVE THE.

FRAME OF CIVIL SOCIETY, TO ARRAY THE LOYAL,

THE SOBER-MINDED AND THE GOOD IN DEFENCE OF THE VENERABLE

CONSTITUTION OF THE BRITISH MONARCHY,

WERE THE DUTIES WHICH, AT THAT AWFUL CRISIS, DEVOLVED UPON
THE BRITISH MINISTER, AND WHICH HE DISCHARGED WITH TRANSCENDENT
ZEAL, INTREPIDITY AND PERSEVERANCE.
HE UPHELD THE NATIONAL HONOUR ABROAD;
HE MAINTAINED AT HOME THE BLESSINGS OF ORDER AND OF TRUE LIBERTY;
AND, IN THE MIDST OF DIFFICULTIES AND PERILS,
HE UNITED AND CONSOLIDATED THE STRENGTH, POWER AND
RESOURCES OF THE EMPIRE.
FOR THESE HIGH PURPOSES, HE WAS GIFTED BY DIVINE PROVIDENCE WITH
ENDOWMENTS RARE IN THEIR SEPARATE EXCELLENCE;
WONDERFUL IN THEIR COMBINATION;
JUDGMENT; IMAGINATION; MEMORY; WIT; FORCE AND ACUTENESS OF REASONING;
ELOQUENCE, COPIOUS AND ACCURATE, COMMANDING AND PERSUASIVE,
AND SUITED FROM ITS SPLENDOUR TO THE DIGNITY OF HIS MIND
AND TO THE AUTHORITY OF HIS STATION;
A LOFTY SPIRIT; A MILD AND INGENUOUS TEMPER.
WARM AND STEDFAST IN FRIENDSHIP, TOWARDS ENEMIES HE WAS
FORBEARING AND FORGIVING.
HIS INDUSTRY WAS NOT RELAXED BY CONFIDENCE IN HIS GREAT ABILITIES
HIS INDULGENCE TO OTHERS WAS NOT ABATED BY THE CONSCIOUSNESS
OF HIS OWN SUPERIORITY;
HIS AMBITION WAS PURE FROM ALL SELFISH MOTIVES;
THE LOVE OF POWER AND THE PASSION OF FAME WERE IN HIM
SUBORDINATE TO VIEWS OF PUBLICK UTILITY;
DISPENSING FOR NEAR TWENTY YEARS THE FAVOURS OF THE CROWN,
HE LIVED WITHOUT OSTENTATION; AND HE DIED POOR.

A GRATEFUL NATION
DECREED TO HIM THOSE FUNERAL HONOURS
WHICH ARE RESERVED FOR EMINENT AND EXTRAORDINARY MEN.

THIS MONUMENT

IS ERECTED BY THE LORD MAYOR, ALDERMEN, AND COMMON COUNCIL,
TO RECORD THE REVERENT AND AFFECTIONATE REGRET
WITH WHICH THE CITY OF LONDON CHERISHES HIS MEMORY;
AND TO HOLD OUT TO THE IMITATION OF POSTERITY
THOSE PRINCIPLES OF PUBLICK AND PRIVATE VIRTUE, WHICH ENSURE
TO NATIONS A SOLID GREATNESS AND TO INDIVIDUALS AN IMPERISHABLE
NAME.

Photo by the L. S. & P. Co., Ltd.

THE GALLERY AND SCREEN

at the west-end of the hall were erected in 1864 from the designs of Mr. (afterwards Sir Horace) Jones, the City Architect. At the same time, the roof was restored and other important alterations carried out, among which was the removal of small galleries over the north and south doorways. The screen is formed of open panels, on a solid base, and with doorway openings. The open work is all finished with arched heads and mouldings, and divided by pillars, with caps and bases which carry the cantilevers, &c. These support a pierced ornamental parapet or balcony front with a projecting centre (in which is placed a clock), with moulded and embattled strings and capping and carried by corbelling and bracketing, all of oak. As will be seen by the illustration, two huge carved figures stand on octagonal pedestals at each angle of the wall. These are the world-renowned giants, GOG AND MAGOG, who are so closely associated with the Guildhall that some

E

THE GIANT GOG.

Photo. by the L. S. & P. Co., Ld.

account of them must be given. Their predecessors, in days
gone by, used to be carried in the processional pageant on
Lord Mayor's Day. It is presumed that they were intended
to represent Gogmagog and Corineus who, in the mythical
chronicles of the monks of the middle ages, are represented

Photo. by the L. S. & P. Co., Ld.

THE GIANT MAGOG.

as fighting the battles of the Trojan invaders against the early inhabitants of this island. In the course of ages, the name of one of the warriors has been forgotten, and the name of the other divided between the two. This myth fostered the belief that these figures preserve to the present day—the tradition that our City was founded by the invader, and that London, as stately "Troynovaunt," or New Troy, was the principal city of Albion, a thousand years before the Christian Era.

The figures in the gallery are both 14 ft. 6 in. in height. The one on the left, Gog, is armed with a globe full of spikes, fastened to a long pole by a chain—a weapon known in the middle ages as "a morning star." In addition, he carries at his back a bow and a quiver full of arrows. The other, Magog, is armed with a shield and spear, and is attired in the old conventional Roman costume so much in fashion at the time when these figures were manufactured. The heads of both are wreathed with laurel.

In a book by one Thomas Boreham (published 1750) we read the following quaint account of them :—

" Before the present giants inhabited Guildhall there were two giants, made only of wicker-work and pasteboard, put together with great art and ingenuity, and these two terrible, original giants had the honour to yearly grace My Lord Mayor's Show, being carried in great triumph in the time of the pageants; and when that eminent annual service was over, remounted their old stations in Guildhall, till, by reason of their very great age, Old Time with the help of the City rats and mice had eaten up all their entrails. The dissolution of the two old, weak and feeble giants gave birth to the two present substantial and majestic giants, who, by order and at the City's charge, were formed and fashioned. Captain Richard Saunders, an eminent carver in King Street, Cheapside, was their father, who after he had completely finished, clothed, and armed these, his two sons, they were immediately advanced to their lofty stations in Guildhall, which they have peacefully enjoyed ever since the year 1708."

The City's accounts show that Captain Saunders was paid £70 for the work. One Richard Saunders ("A train-band Captain eke was he, of famous London Town "), was paid for the execution of the beautiful carving in the Church of St. Giles, Cripplegate, in 1705. Possibly, the carvings of other City churches were produced in his workshop, and, may it be said, are now attributed to a man of greater fame.

The Court of Husting.

THIS Court, or, more correctly speaking, these Courts : the Court of Husting of Pleas of Land and the Court of Husting of Common Pleas are certainly of Anglo-Saxon, if not of Scandinavian, origin, for the laws of Edward the Confessor directed the Sittings thereof to take place alternately every week. The term "Husting" signifies "a Court held in a house," in contradistinction to other Courts, which, in Saxon times, were usually held in the open air.

The Court of Husting was, originally, the County Court of the City, which was always a County of itself. It is the oldest Court of Record within the City, and was the sole Court for settling disputes between the citizens. About the time of Edward 1. actions merely personal, came to be decided in the Mayor's Court and the Sheriffs' Courts, whilst all real and mixed actions, with the exception of actions of ejectment, remained subject to the exclusive jurisdiction of the Court of Husting, as before. An appeal from the Court of Husting originally lay to the Court of St. Martin-le-Grand, now practically obsolete, composed of a Commission of Judges of the High Court, who originally sat at St. Martin-le-Grand, but, since the time of Henry VIII., at Guildhall, and from which Court an appeal lay to the House of Lords. A portion of the jurisdiction originally exercised by the Court of Husting was transferred to the Mayor's Court. The Courts are held on the raised dais at the east end of the Hall, called the Hustings, by the Lord Mayor, Aldermen and Sheriffs, who are the Judges, with the Recorder sitting as Assessor to pronounce the judgment of the Court.

The Common Hall.

A COMMON HALL, as mentioned in different parts of this book, may be briefly described as an assembly of the Members of the various " Livery Companies " of the City. In addition to the Common Hall on Midsummer Day, for electing Sheriffs, and that on Michaelmas Day for the election of Lord Mayor, Common Halls are also held in the Guildhall in times of trouble and discontent, when the opinions of the citizens require to be expressed. The full title of the Common Hall is "The Meeting or Assembly of the Mayor, Aldermen, and Liverymen of the several Companies of the City of London in Common Hall assembled." There are 76 Companies or Guilds in the City, containing about 8,800 Members who are Liverymen and Freemen of the City, and in consequence of their social status and numbers, their influence has always been very great. A Common Hall is summoned by the Lord Mayor, who presides, and is attended by the Aldermen, Sheriffs, and High Officers, in full state.

Public Meetings in the Hall.

THIS magnificent Hall is not used merely for meetings connected with Corporation elections, ceremonials and festivities. By permission of the Lord Mayor and Common Council, meetings of public interest and importance are held here, on various questions interesting to the country at large as well as the City. Among these may be mentioned Parliamentary Reform, Religious Equality, National Defence, Popular Education, &c. The Hall has also witnessed many a stirring scene in the Election of Members of Parliament for the City.

Not the least interesting of the meetings held here is the Annual Banquet to Poor Children, usually given about Christmas-tide. This had its origin in 1893, when in January of that year, Sir Stuart Knill, Bart., as Lord Mayor, invited the children attending the various Ward Schools of the City, to dinner at the Guildhall. Every year since a similar dinner and entertainment has been given to the poor children of the Metropolis. The children are selected through the agency of the Ragged School Union. Over 1,200 were entertained at dinner last Christmas time in the Hall, while hampers containing meat, pies, cakes, sweets, &c., were sent to nearly 5,000 crippled children who were unable to be present. Year by year, this entertainment has been promoted by Mr. Alderman Treloar, the expense connected therewith being defrayed by subscriptions of members of the Corporation, of the Livery Companies, and of other friends interested in the welfare of the poor.

Leaving the Hall by the Archway on the north side (over which hangs the "Elcho Challenge Shield" won by the English team at Bisley, four years in succession, viz., 1895, 1896, 1897 and 1898) and after mounting a short flight of steps, we

Photo. by the L. S. y P. Co., Ld.

ARCHWAY LEADING TO THE LOBBY.

are on the way to the Council Chamber, the Aldermen's Court Room, and the various Committee Rooms. Passing into the ante-lobby, we see on the left the offices of the 'Keeper of the Guildhall,' an office of great responsibility, involving as it does, not only the general charge of the Guildhall itself, and its many Courts and Committee Rooms, but also special charge for their order and cleanliness, and for the safety of the entire building at night ; for this reason he resides in a suite of apartments in the Guildhall, and is thus personally able to superintend the Beadles, Firemen, and Watchmen acting under his directions. At all Meetings of the Common Hall, Court of Common Council, and of its many Committees, the Keeper of the Guildhall is always in attendance either personally or by deputy, and on Corporation visits to the Queen, or any Member of the Royal Family, he attends, and is responsible that no strangers intrude upon the Royal presence. He also issues notices for all meetings of the Corporation and its Committees, and has a large staff of assistants to enable him to carry out this work. Among the numerous accounts kept by him are the expenses incurred in the watching of the Guildhall, the expenditure of the allowances to Committees, the payment of pensions to certain retired prison and other officials.

The Ante-Lobby.

THE Ante-Lobby is painted to symbolize the armorial bearings of the City, and of the Livery Companies. On the north wall are pictured St. George and St. Paul, the patrons of the City. The former having conquered the dragon,

Photo. by the L. S. & P. Co.,

THE LOBBY AND ENTRANCE TO THE COUNCIL CHAMBER.

emblematical of the evil principle, the princess, kneeling in the background, represents the good principle ; while on the walls of the City, are arrayed her parents and relations, in the persons of the Lord Mayor, Sheriffs, Aldermen, Commoners, and citizens. St. Paul, standing in front of the old Cathedral, offers his red Sword of martyrdom, which is placed in the first quarter of the City arms.

On the west wall is pictured the City herself, in livery gown, seated in the midst of her gates : old London Bridge, with a water pageant, being in front. On the east wall is the City arms ; which is the plain red cross of St. George with the Sword of St. Paul ; the sinister wing of a Dragon for crest, and the conquered Dragon made to act as the supporter ; the whole surrounded by the arms of the twelve great Livery Companies. On the south wall arises the heraldic tree, carrying the arms of all the smaller Companies, which continue also as a border round the whole design. This work was executed in 1889, under the superintendence, and at the expense of the late Alderman Sir Stuart Knill, Bart., LL.D.

In this Ante-Lobby are placed marble busts of well-known soldiers and philanthropists, Granville Sharp (1824), *Chantrey* ; Thomas Clarkson (1839), *Behnes* ; Sir Henry Havelock of Indian Mutiny fame (1858), *Behnes* ; General Gordon the martyred hero of Khartoum (1886), *Theed* ; and the Earl of Shaftesbury (1886), *Merrett*. The first two were the earliest advocates for the abolition of slavery ; on the back of "Sharp's" bust is this inscription :—

"To whom England owes the glorious verdict of her highest Court of Law, that the slave who sets his feet on British ground, becomes, at that instant, free."

Passing through a pair of handsome doors we enter the
Lobby of the Council Chamber.

The illustration on the preceding page gives a good general idea of its appearance.

Marble busts of distinguished statesmen, whom the Corporation has been proud to honour, are placed around:— Lord Canning (1864), *Noble* ; Viscount Palmerston (1867), *Durham* ; Lord Brougham (1869), *Adams* ; Richard Cobden (1869), *Noble* ; Earl Derby ('the Rupert of Debate') (1871), *Noble* ; Earl of Beaconsfield (1882), *Belt* ; W. E. Gladstone

Photo. by the L. S. & P. Co., Ltd.

NELSON.   GORDON.   TENNYSON.   HAVELOCK.   WELLINGTON.

THE "PEN AND THE SWORD."

(The busts of Nelson, Tennyson and Wellington are in the Art Gallery.)

(1882), *Woolner* ; Earl Russell (1883), *Birch* ; Earl of Iddesleigh (1887), *Tyler* ; W. H. Smith (1892), *Whitehead*. A bust of the Marquis of Salisbury (1886) by *Bruce Joy*, is in the Mansion House. On the walls are portraits of four of the Judges who arranged the fire claims (1668-72), Sir William Ellys, Sir Francis North, Sir Timothy Lyttleton, Sir Robert Atkyns, and of Lord Denman, Common Serjeant (1822), and

Lord Chief Justice of the King's Bench. On the right is a painting by Ralph Dodd, representing George III. on the occasion of his Thanksgiving visit to St. Paul's on recovery from his illness (1789), receiving from the Lord Mayor the City's sword at Temple Bar. This was formerly used as a screen in the Mansion House.

Photo. by the L. S. & P. Co.,

BROUGHAM. RUSSELL. BEACONSFIELD PALMERSTON. GLADSTONE.

STATESMEN.

Opposite is a painting representing King Louis Phillipe receiving at Windsor Castle an address of congratulation from the Lord Mayor and a deputation from the Common Council, October 12th, 1844. This picture was presented to the Corporation by the French King himself. Underneath is hung a key to the different figures.

On the left of the Lobby is the Members' Reading-room, the walls of which are covered with portraits of Lord Mayors and others who have taken part in the work of the Corporation. On the right, approached by an easy flight of steps, on the top of which are a handsome pair of brass gates, is

The Council Chamber.

IT does not appear that there is any record extant of a particular chamber being set apart for the deliberation of the Common Council earlier than that recorded by Stow, who, speaking of Guildhall and the foundation of the Mayor's Court as being laid in the reign of Henry VI., (1424) says, " *Then was built the Maior's Chamber and the Counsell Chamber with other rooms above the staires.*" The next mention of a new Council Chamber is found in the City's own records ; the entry is dated 15th October, 1605, and is as follows :—

" ITEM :—It is ordered that Sir Henry Billingesley, Sir William Ryder, Sir John Garrard, Sir Thomas Bennett, Sir Thomas Cambell, Sir William Romney, Sir John Swynnerton, Knights ; and Mr. Sword-Bearer, do attend them ; calling unto them the Cittyes Workmen, and such others as they shall think fitt ; shall consider of a convenient place to be had for erection of a faire Councell Chamber for the Lord Maior and his bretheren the Aldermen, and the learned Councell and officers of this Cittye to meet in ; and for the enlargement of the Threasorye for keeping the Cittyes Chres. and Records, within the carpenters' yard on the north syde of their Councell Chamber, and to make report to this Court of their opinions therein, and Thomas Harvest to warne them."

The Committee thus appointed no doubt reported to the Court in due course, but several years elapsed before the building was commenced ; for it was not until the year 1614 that the Council commenced to use their new chamber. Here they continued to sit until the erection of what we now know as the " Old Council Chamber " in 1777, and of which an illustration is given (page 92). The Chamber above referred to as being built in 1614 adjoined the north wall of the Great Hall, the site forming a considerable portion of the south-east area of the existing new Council Chamber. This Chamber was approached from the Hall by steps situated where the monument of the Duke of Wellington is now placed. In this Chamber both King James I. and his ill-fated son Charles appeared before the Common Council, as we have described elsewhere, and where the latter was so coldly received.

During the 150 years that this Chamber was used, many distinguished men occupied the Mayoral chair. The first was Sir Thomas Myddelton, who, on the day of his election (September 29th, 1613), presided at the ceremony of the opening of the New River, which had been constructed by his brother, Sir Hugh. Among others may be mentioned Sir John Swynnerton (one of the committee for viewing the site) Alderman of Cripplegate, who entertained the Count Palatine when he came over to be betrothed to Elizabeth, the daughter of James I. ; Sir William Cockayne, the first Governor of the Irish Society ; Sir Edward Barkham, whose grandson, Sir Robert Walpole, was Prime Minister in the reigns of the first two Georges ; and many others.

Within this Hall, many stirring debates and scenes took place, notably during the Civil War, at the Restoration, the Revolution, and in the next century, during the early part of the long struggle for the liberties both of the subject and of the press. The first stone of the present

Council Chamber

WAS laid on the 30th of April, 1883, and the first meeting within its walls was held on the 2nd of October, 1884. It was built from the designs and under the superintendence of Sir Horace Jones, P.R.I.B.A., the City Architect, upon the north side of the Guildhall, and upon the site formerly occupied by the old Court of Exchequer, the Chamberlain's, Town Clerk's and Architect's Offices.

Arranged round the corridor are marble busts of some of
those whom their fellow-citizens have delighted to honour for
their devotion to the interests of the City, for their attention
to its municipal affairs, and for their personal influence with
those who came into contact with them.   There are busts of
Alderman Sir B. S. Phillips, *Merrett* (1885); Alderman Sir R.
Carden, Bart., *Merrett* (1886); Alderman Sir A. Lusk, Bart.,
McCarthy (1888); Alderman Sir R. Fowler, Bart., *Merrett* (1891);
Benjamin Scott, City Chamberlain, *Merrett* (1892); Alderman
Sir Polydore De Keyser, *Johnson* (1893), ; Sir J. B. Monckton,
Town Clerk, *Raemakers* (1894).   A marble bust of H.R.H.
The Duke of Cambridge, *Williamson* (1897) also stands here.

It will be seen from the illustration, that the building is
duodecagonal in design.   It is 54 feet in diameter, surrounded
by a corridor 9 feet wide, above which is a gallery for the
accommodation of the public and the press.   The height
from the floor to the dome is 61 feet 6 inches ; above this rises
an oak lantern, the top of which is 81 feet 6 inches ; this lights
and ventilates the entire chamber.   The entrance for the Lord
Mayor and Aldermen is at the east end behind the chair,
for the Members of the Common Council from the lobby and
corridor, and for the public from Basinghall Street.

There is sitting accommodation for the Lord Mayor, 25
Aldermen, Recorder and Sheriffs, and 206 Common Councilmen, in addition to the High Officers and the Clerks, who sit
at the table below the dais.   Special seats are provided for
Chairmen of Committees.   Division gangways run north and
south of the chamber.

The materials used in the construction of the building are
Bath and Portland stone for the windows and dressings, &c.
The walls are faced externally with Kentish rag.   The columns
and arches of the arcade are in polished Hopton Wood stone.
The interior of the Dome is parcelled out by massive oak ribs,
traceried lunettes, and twelve three-light clerestory windows,
the central lights being filled in with figure subjects, representing

the cardinal virtues ; the panels immediately above these windows have artistic Frescoes representing the various trades and crafts of the following Livery Companies, with their Arms above tastefully placed in the lunettes. The Companies represented are the Armourers, Bakers, Barbers, Brewers, Brasiers, Clothworkers, Cutlers, Drapers, Dyers, Fishmongers, Girdlers, Goldsmiths, Grocers, Haberdashers, Ironmongers, Leathersellers, Mercers, Merchant-Taylors, Pewterers, Salters, Skinners, Tallow Chandlers, Vintners and Wax Chandlers. On the panels of either side of the windows are represented the flowers and fruits of the several months of the year, together with the signs of the Zodiac. The building is lighted by an elaborate gilt pendant chandelier and brass standard lights, fitted originally for gas, but now with the electric light, which was installed in 1889.

The twelve richly-canopied carved screens, which divide the chamber from the corridor, are executed in wainscot glazed with ornamental lead-lights, having the Arms of the various Companies, viz.: Apothecaries, Basket-makers, Blacksmiths, Bowyers, Broderers, Butchers, Carpenters, Clockmakers, Coachmakers, Cooks, Coopers, Cordwainers, Curriers, Distillers, Fanmakers, Farriers, Feltmakers, Fletchers, Founders, Framework Knitters, Fruiterers, Glass Sellers, Glaziers, Glovers, Gold and Silver Wire Drawers, Gunmakers, Horners, Inn-Holders, Joiners, Loriners, Makers of Playing Cards, Masons, Musicians, Needle Makers, Painter Stainers, Parish Clerks, Patten-makers, Plasterers, Plumbers, Poulters, Saddlers, Scriveners, Shipwrights, Spectacle-makers, Stationers, Tinplate Workers, Turners, Tylers and Bricklayers, Upholders, Weavers, Wheelwrights and Woolmen. In the four niches have been placed marble busts of Her Majesty, the Queen (1855) and H.R.H. the late Prince Consort (1862) both by Joseph Durham, and their Royal Highnesses the Prince and Princess of Wales by Marshall Wood (1863) and C. E. Van

Derbosch (1871) respectively. Behind the Lord Mayor's Seat is a statue of George III, the work of Chantrey on the commission of the Corporation, at a cost of £3,089, and placed (1815) in the Old Council Chamber in token of their sense of the King's "endearing and amiable qualities," whence on the opening of this chamber it was removed to its present site. On the left of the Lord Mayor's seat is seen, on one of the pillars, a commemorative tablet inscribed as follows :—

ON THIS SITE STOOD
THE COUNCIL CHAMBER
(BUILT 1614, VACATED 1777, BURNT 1786),
WHEREIN CHARLES I. CAME TO DEMAND THE SURRENDER
OF THE FIVE MEMBERS OF PARLIAMENT,
ON THE 5TH JANUARY, 1641-2.

THIS RECORD IS PLACED
BY ORDER OF THE COMMON COUNCIL
OF THE 24TH JULY, 1890,
ON THE REPORT OF ITS LIBRARY COMMITTEE.

This incident has also been commemorated (1897) by a painting on panel in the ambulatory of the Royal Exchange.

It has been customary for many years, to show special respect to a Lord Mayor, on taking his seat in the Council Chamber for the first time, by the members of the Court of Common Council appearing in full official costume—the Aldermen in scarlet, and the Commoners in mazarine blue gowns. On taking his seat, the Lord Mayor addresses the Court, expressing his confidence that the members of the Court will, with their usual courtesy and good feeling, assist him in his duties in the chair, and abide by his ruling in matters of order, to which the "Chief Commoner," on behalf of the Court, makes a suitable reply. It may truly be said that the confidence the Lord Mayor places in the Court is seldom, if ever, misplaced.

The illustration shows the scene in the Court immediately after the Lord Mayor's opening address.

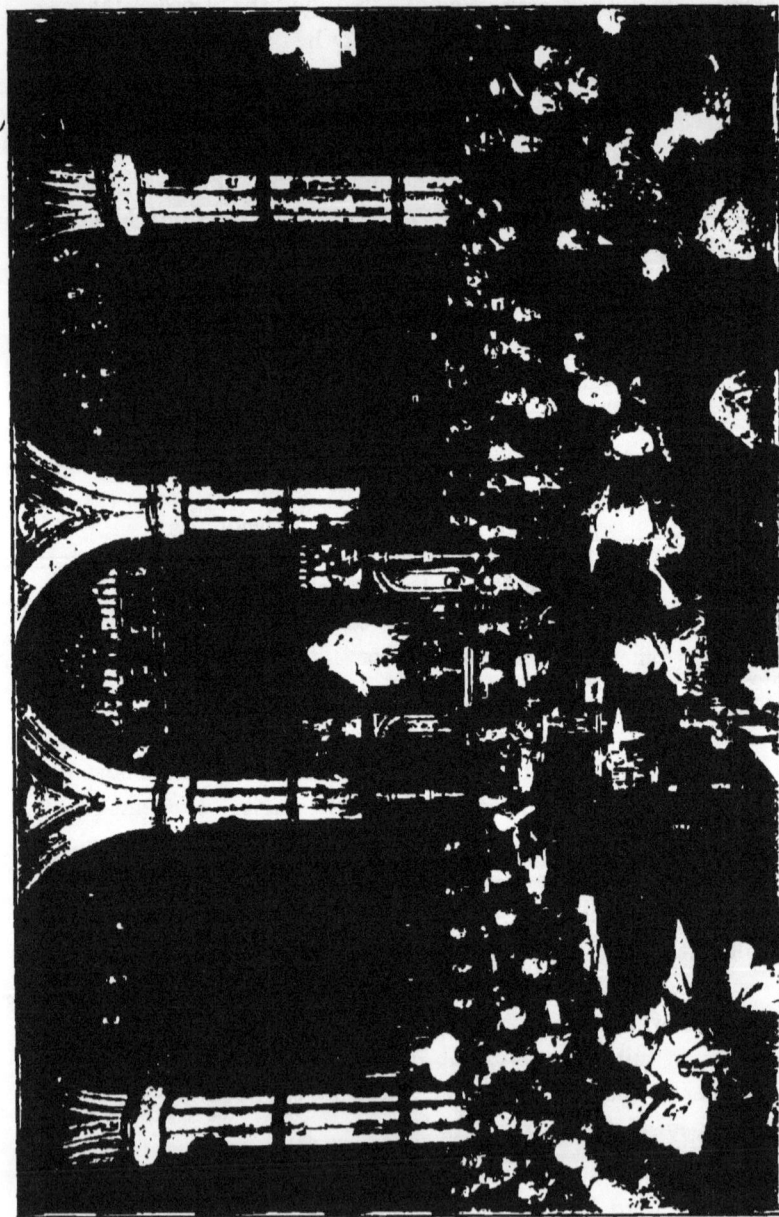

Photo. by the L. S. & P. Co. Ltd.

THE COUNCIL CHAMBER. THE FIRST MEETING AFTER LORD MAYOR'S DAY, 1897.

Leaving the Council Chamber we pass to the end of the vestibule ; on the left is the approach to the offices of the Chamberlain, the Town Clerk, and the Surveyor, and also to the various Committee Rooms. Several of the minor Livery Companies who have no Hall of their own are allowed to transact their business in one of these rooms. In the centre is the door (surmounted by a unique clock) leading to the Aldermen's Room, that, on the right, leads to the new offices of the Public Health Department, the public entrance to which is in Basinghall Street. These offices have been erected at a cost of £20,000, and the staff of the Department have just entered in occupation.

ᵀ⁣ʰₑ ᴬldermen's ℭourt ℜoom.

ᵀHIS room may be appropriately described as the "Gilded Chamber ;" as it is certainly the most sumptuously decorated and attractive apartment in the Guildhall. The room itself was probably built in the early part of the 17th century, and with other portions of the Guildhall suffered in the Great Fire of 1666. It was restored within a few years. By comparing the decorative work of the ceiling, the shields in the cornice, the City Arms, and the style of the doorways, with similar work to be seen in some of the Livery Companies' Halls (that were restored soon after the Fire), the date may be fairly ascribed to the years 1670-80. The gilded borderings and the modellings of the quaint designs of animals and foliage are rich and tasteful, and must have been executed by an artist of exceptional ability. The paintings, added in 1727, were executed and presented by Sir James Thornhill, who also presented the painting over the black marble chimney-piece. The Corporation, in acknowledgment of his kindness, presented him with a gold cup of the value of £225. The painting in the centre of the ceiling, enclosed within an oval border, is intended to typify the old traditions of the city. The seated figure represents London, she wears a mural crown, and in her left hand grasps the civic shield. The figure behind is intended for Pallas, the daughter of Jupiter, and beneath her two little boys, one bearing upon his shoulder the City Sword, the other pointing to the Cap of Maintenance and the Mace that lie beneath her feet. There is an allegorical figure of Peace, who is represented as presenting an olive branch, and another figure of Plenty pouring out riches from her horn. There are two oblong compartments at each end of the ceiling, they contain youthful figures representative of the cardinal virtues, Prudence, Temperance, Justice, and Fortitude. The painting over the chimney-piece typifies London, Justice, Liberty and Truth. Over the door facing the Lord Mayor's chair appears the motto, " *Audi alteram partem*," one most appropriate when the purposes, to which the room is devoted, are considered ; over this is a full City Arms, of which the following is a heraldic description :—Arms. *Argent*, a cross *gules*, in the first quarter a sword in pale, point upwards, of the last. Crest, a dragon's sinister wing *argent*, charged with a cross *gules*. Supporters, on either side a dragon with wings elevated and endorsed, *argent* and charged on the wings with a cross *gules*. Motto, " *Domine dirige nos.*"

A Peer's Helmet with lambrequins is also depicted resting on the shield. *It may be mentioned that the use of a Crest and Supporters to the City Arms is comparatively modern—probably the Arms in this room is one of the earliest examples of these additions to the simple shield.*

The shields in the cornice surrounding the chamber (twenty-eight in all) were possibly intended to contain the Arms of the twenty-six Aldermen and the two Sheriffs, but we have no means of definitely ascertaining whose Arms were originally painted thereon.

THE ALDERMEN'S ROOM.

Photo. by the L. S. & P. Co. Ld.

In 1807 the room seems to have been re-embellished, and the Arms of all the Aldermen who had served the office of Mayor, and who were then living, painted on the shields, the only exception being the Arms of Sir Watkin Lewes—who was Mayor in 1780, and who died in 1805—this shield is in the south-west corner; the Arms of Nathaniel Newnham—who was Mayor, 1782, and who died in 1810—occupying the corresponding position in the opposite corner. The fourteen remaining vacant shields were afterwards filled in, as we see them now, with the Arms of successive Lord Mayors.

The following list gives the names and date of election of the Mayors whose Arms surround the cornice :—Sir Watkin Lewes, 1780; Nathaniel Newnham, 1782; Sir William Curtis, Bart., 1795; Sir Brook Watson, Bart., 1796; Sir John Wm. Anderson, Bart., 1797; Sir Richard Carr Glynn, Bart., 1798; Harvey Christian Combe, 1799; Sir William Staines, 1800; Sir John Eamer, 1801; Sir Charles Price, Bart., 1802; Sir John Perring, Bart., 1803; Sir James Shaw, Bart., 1805; Sir William Leighton, 1806; John Ansley, 1807; Sir Charles Flower, 1808; Thomas Smith, 1809; Joshua Jonathan Smith, 1810; Sir Claudius Stephen Hunter, Bart., 1811; George Scholey, 1812; Sir William Domville, Bart, 1813; Samuel Birch, 1814; Sir Matthew Wood, Bart., 1815-16; Christopher Smith, 1817; John Atkins, 1818; George Bridges, 1819; John Thomas Thorpe, 1820; Christopher Magnay, 1821; Sir William Heygate, Bart., 1822.

The Royal Arms over the Chair, was put up at the same time that the 28 shields were commenced to be painted (1807). The Union with Ireland had taken place, as the Irish Harp is in its position in the third quarter of the Arms, and on the Shield are the Arms of Hanover ensigned with the " Electoral Bonnet "; this " Bonnet " was only in use in England in connection with the Arms between 1801 and 1816. After this time until the death of William IV. the Royal Crown took its place.

This Royal Arms is believed to be perfectly unique, and probably nowhere else in the Kingdom is there a Royal Arms in an official position, charged with the Arms of Hanover ensigned with the Electoral " Bonnet."

An heraldic description of these Arms may be found interesting. It is as follows :—Per pale and per chevron (1) *gules*, two lions of England for Brunswick ; (2) *or*, semée of hearts a lion rampant *azure*, for Lunenburg ; (3) *gules*, a horse courant, *argent*, for Westphalia ; (4) over all on an inescutcheon *gules*, the golden crown of Charlemagne.

It is probable that, in 1823, the windows behind the chair were remodelled, and the various Arms commenced to be painted on the glass, and continued year by year, until all the panes were full ; as was also the case in later years with the windows in the north-east corner of the room. The windows behind the chair contain the Arms of Robert Waithman, elected 1823 ; John Garratt, 1824 ; William Venables, 1825 ; Anthony Brown, 1826 ; Matthias Prime Lucas, 1827 ; William Thompson, 1828 ; John Crowder, 1829 ; Sir John Key, Bart., 1830-1 ; Sir Peter Laurie, 1832 ; Charles Farebrother, 1833 ; Henry Winchester, 1834 ; Wm. Taylor Copeland, 1835 ; Thomas Kelly, 1836 ; Sir John Cowan, Bart., 1837 ; Samuel Wilson, 1838 ; Sir Chapman Marshall, 1839. The large window opposite the chimney piece contains the arms of Thomas Johnson, 1840 ; Sir John Pirie, Bart., 1841 ; John Humphery, 1842 ; Sir William Magnay, Bart., 1843 ; Michael Gibbs, 1844 ; John Johnson, 1845 ; Sir George Carroll, 1846 ; Jno. Kinnersley Hooper, 1847 ; Sir James Duke, Bart., 1848 ; Thomas Farncomb, 1849 ; Sir John Musgrove, Bart., 1850 ; William Hunter, 1851 ; Thomas Challis, 1852 ; Thomas Sidney, 1853 ; Sir Francis G. Moon, Bart., 1854 ; David Salomons, 1855 ; T. Quested Finnis, 1856 ; Sir Robert W. Carden, 1857 ; David Williams Wire, 1858 ; John Carter, 1859 ; William Cubitt, 1860-1 ; W. Anderson Rose, 1862 ; William

Lawrence, 1863 ; Warren S. Hale, 1864. The window overhead contains the Arms of Benjamin Samuel Phillips, 1865 ; Sir Thomas Gabriel, Bart, 1866 ; William Ferneley Allen, 1867 ; James Clarke Lawrence, 1868 ; Robert Besley, 1869 ; Thomas Dakin, 1870 ; Sir Sills J. Gibbons, Bart., 1871 ; Sir Sydney H. Waterlow, 1872 ; Sir Andrew Lusk, Bart., 1873. On either side the entrance at the east end of the Chamber are six panels carved in wood, each of a different design. On these panels are the Arms of David H. Stone, 1874 ; W. J. R. Cotton, 1875 ; Sir Thomas White, 1876 ; Sir T. S. Owden, 1877 ; Sir Charles Whetham, 1878; Sir Francis W. Truscott, 1879 ; Sir William McArthur, K.C.M.G., 1880 ; Sir J. Whittaker Ellis, Bart., 1881 ; Sir Henry E. Knight, 1882 ; Robert Nicholas Fowler, 1883-85 ; George S. Nottage, 1884 ; Sir John Staples, K.C.M.G., 1885.

On the right of the Chair, is a series of carved panels of the same character as those just described, containing the Arms of Sir Reginald Hanson, Bart., 1886 ; Sir Polydore De Keyser, 1887 ; Sir J. Whitehead, Bart., 1888 ; Sir Henry Isaacs, 1889 ; Sir Joseph Savory, Bart., 1890 ; Sir David Evans, K.C.M.G., 1891 ; Sir Stuart Knill, Bart., 1892 ; Sir George Tyler, Bart., 1893 ; Sir Joseph Renals, Bart., 1894 ; Sir Walter Wilkin, K.C.M.G., 1895 ; Sir George F. Faudel-Phillips, Bart., G.C.I.E., 1896 ; Sir Horatio David Davies, K.C.M.G., 1897. There are nine vacant panels, on which will be painted the Arms of future Lord Mayors. Immediately over the Lord Mayor's seat is the rest for the Sword of State. In front of the chair is a table, around which sit the principal officers of the Court. The seats for the twenty-five other Aldermen, the Recorder, and the two Sheriffs are placed round the Chamber. The seats are allotted according to seniority—the Senior Aldermen sitting on the left of the Lord Mayor, the Recorder sitting on the immediate right, and the other Aldermen on the right and left, according to seniority. The Sheriffs sit, one at either side, at the end of the rows of seats.

The Old Council Chamber.

THE Vestibule of the Old Council Chamber is approached through the doors at the end of the Lobby. On entering the Chamber one is struck by its handsome proportions and excellent lighting. On the walls are hung portraits of distinguished personages, including those of some of the Judges who settled the claims and contentions incident on the rebuilding of the City after the Great Fire of 1666, these were painted by Joseph Michael Wright, on the commission of the Common Council. The resolution of the Court runs as follows:—

"That in contemplation of the favour and kindness of the Right Hon. Sir H. Bridgman, Lord Chancellor and Keeper of the Great Seal of England, the Justices of the King's Bench and Common Pleas, and Barons of the Exchequer, to the State of the Citty, in and about the Act of Parliament, and in consideration of its instituting a Judicature for determining of discussions between landlord and tenant, the Court doth think fit, and order that their pictures be taken by a skilful hand, and be kept in some public place of the City for a grateful memorial of their good offices."

These portraits were originally hung in the Great Hall (1673). Afterwards, for many years, they adorned the Courts of Queen's Bench and Common Pleas, when these Courts sat at Guildhall. By a singular coincidence, the Chamber in which these portraits hang, has witnessed—December 1897—an inquiry respecting the greatest fire (that in Cripplegate) that has occurred in the City since the Great Fire of 1666. The Judges represented are Sir Edward Atkyns, Sir Orlando Bridgman, Sir Matthew Hale, Sir John Kelynge, Sir William Morton,

Sir Heneage Finch, Earl of Nottingham, Solicitor-General, and afterwards Lord Chancellor—Sir Richard Rainsford, Sir Christopher Turnor, Sir Edward Turnor, Sir Thomas Twysden, Sir John Vaughan, Sir Hugh Wyndham, and Sir Wadham Wyndham. The portrait of George III. is by Allan Ramsay, the others are of the Czar Nicholas I. of Russia, the Czarewitch, afterwards Alexander II., and the Empress Catherine.

THE OLD COUNCIL CHAMBER, 1777-1884.

The portrait of Sir David Salomons is specially interesting from the fact that he was the first Lord Mayor (1855-6) of the Jewish faith. Marble busts adorn the Chamber, of R. Lambert Jones, *Behnes* (1847); T. H. Hall, *Durham* (1857); J. B. Bunning, City Architect, *Durham* (1874); Russell Gurney, Q.C., M.P., Recorder, 1856 to 1878, *MacCarthy* (1883). As will be noted, the room is fitted up as a Court of Law,

and is now usually used for the sittings of the Mayor's
Court, or more properly speaking, "the Court of our Sovereign
Lady the Queen, holden before the Mayor and Aldermen of the
City of London." The Lord Mayor and the Aldermen are
the nominal Judges; the Recorder sitting by custom as
the sole Judge ; but, in his absence, the Common Sergeant
presides as Judge.

This Chamber was erected by George Dance, the City
Architect, and stands on a part of the garden of the then
Town Clerk's House—replacing the Chamber erected (for the
Mayor's Court) in 1424. The meetings of the Common Council
were first held here about the year 1777, and the Chamber built
in 1614 was soon afterwards demolished. Like its predecessor,
this Chamber has witnessed many a stirring scene ; most of the
Honorary Freedoms have been voted and presented here, as
well as addresses to Royal and distinguished persons. Here stood,
as recipients of the City's Freedom, Nelson, Rodney, Hood,
Duncan, Howe, Pitt the younger, Beresford, Wellington,
Brougham, Peel, Colin Campbell, Rajah Brooke, Outram, Russell,
Disraeli, Livingstone, Shaftesbury, and many other distinguished men whose names are written in the annals of fame.

In this Chamber have been inaugurated, and carried out,
schemes for most of the great improvements in the Public
Streets that have been effected in the present century. A
few of these may be mentioned, and their cost to the Corporation ;
Approaches to London Bridge North and South of the Thames,
and enlarging the site of the Royal Exchange and its approaches
(£1,250,000) ; formation of Cannon Street (£540,000) ; Holborn
Valley Viaduct and Improvements (£1,715,000) and laying down
Fire Hydrants (£27,000). As a late member of the Common
Council said (in 1884), when formally taking leave of the Old
Chamber, " Here have been fostered and supported those great
charities which are the glory and boast of this old England

of ours,—Almshouses, Asylums, Dispensaries, Hospitals, Infirmaries, Schools, and Societies of many kinds, whose objects are, the removal and relief of poverty and distress."

Returning by the way he came, the visitor should cross the great Hall, and pass through the Porch—outside of which, on the left, is the entrance to

The Art Gallery.

THIS Gallery was established by the Corporation in 1885, and was formally opened free to the public in 1886,— the attendance has averaged 200,000 visitors annually. Many works have been presented to the Gallery since its establishment, among the Donors being the Drapers', Goldsmiths', Salters' and Vintners' Companies, Edward Armitage, Esq., R.A., and Sir John Gilbert, R.A., by whom the Gallery has been enriched by sixteen important works, executed by himself, five being in oil and eleven in water colours. Many pictures have also been bequeathed to the Gallery by private individuals.

Among the more important works are several portraits by Sir Joshua Reynolds ; the "Murder of Rizzio" and the "Assassination of James I. of Scotland" by John Opie ; and the "Death of Wat Tyler" by Northcote ; the picture of the Banquet in the Guildhall when in 1814 the Czar Nicholas of Russia and the King of Prussia attended, painted by William Daniell, R.A. The portrait of H.M. Queen Victoria, presented by herself to the Corporation in 1839, painted by Sir George Hayter. Two examples of David Roberts, "Antwerp Cathedral" and "The interior of the Church of St. Stephen, Vienna" ; Edward Armitage's "Herodias' Daughter," and the oil paintings and drawings presented by Sir John Gilbert, R.A., are all well worthy of attention.

The sculptor's art is represented by a marble statue of Sir Henry Irving (1890) by *Onslow Ford, R.A. ;* marble busts of Wellington (1814) by *P. Turnerelli;* Nelson (1797) by *Hon. Mrs. Damer;* Tennyson (1893) by *Williamson;* the Rev. Henry White, M.A., late Chaplain of the Savoy, (1891), by *T. R. Essex;* and a Statue " Waiting for his Innings," by *Durham, A.R.A.*

In 1890 the Gallery was enlarged, and previous to the re-arrangement therein of the Corporation's own collection, a Loan Exhibition of Pictures was held. It was open to the public for three months, and was visited by 109,000 persons. In 1892 another Exhibition of a similar character was held, and was visited by 236,000. Similar Exhibitions have been held in 1894, 1895, 1896, and 1897—with an aggregate attendance of nearly 1,000,000 persons. At all these Exhibitions the admission was free, and the whole expense defrayed by the Corporation out of its private funds. The object of the Exhibitions was to render accessible to the general public many distinguished works of art from private collections, which would, probably, never have been seen by the bulk of the people, except under the auspices of such a body as the Corporation. Many of the pictures also, which the Corporation were able to place on view, had never before been publicly exhibited, and the opportunity of again seeing many of them in public is remote. The Gallery is open daily, free of charge, from 10 a.m. to 5 p.m.

Passing from the Gallery, the visitor will find himself in the corridor leading (on the right) to the Library. In this corridor will be seen on the walls many rare prints and photographs, and also the large original designs for tapestry by Richard Beavis. The subjects are : " The Solemn Joust on London Bridge, between Scotch and English Champions, David de Lyndesaye, Earl of Crawford, and Lord John de Welles, A.D. 1390," and " Robert Fitz-Walter receiving the City's Banner from the Lord Mayor, on the steps of St. Paul's Cathedral, A.D. 1250." These tapestries, with two other subjects ordered by the Corporation at a cost of £1,405 from the Windsor Tapestry Works, now hang in the Mansion House. At the top of the flight of steps, on the right, is a stone statue of Charles II., and, on the left, one of Sir John Cutler, a benefactor of the College of Physicians. These statues were erected on the façade of the old College in Warwick Lane, built by Wren in 1680, and were presented to the Corporation when that building was demolished in 1873. Facing the visitor is the Newspaper Room and the entrance to

The Library.

THE first mention of a Library at the Guildhall is contained in the following extracts from the records of the Corporation, the original being in Latin :—

"Item the same day [to wit the 27th September, A° 4 Henry VI., 1425] it was granted by the said Mayor and Aldermen and Commonalty that the new House or Library, which the said executors [to wit of the testament of Richard Whityngton] and the executors of William Bury made near the Guildhall, and the custody of the same, together with the chambers built underneath the same, should be in the disposition and management of the said executors ; in such manner that all and everything, which the same executors should think fit to ordain touching the placing the books or doing other matters, shall be done and executed as fully and perfectly as if they had been ordained by the said Mayor, Aldermen, and Commonalty."

The building thus erected was a separate structure, situated on the south side of the Guildhall Chapel ; it is described in a schedule of the possessions of the Guildhall College, dated 24th July, 1549, 3 Edward VI.,

"as a certen house nexte unto the sam Chapell apperteynyng called the Library, all waies res'ved for students to resorte unto, w¹ three chambres under nithe the saide library, which library being covered w¹ Slate is valued together w¹ the Chambres at xiijs. iiijd. yearly."

From the same document we learn that

"the saied library is a house appointed by the saied Maior and cominalitie for. . . resorte of all students for their education in Divine Scriptures."

The noble liberality of Richard Whitington and William Bury, the founders of the Library, was well supported by Whitington's executor, John Carpenter, the learned Common Clerk, compiler of the "Liber Albus" and founder of the City of London School, who left, by his will,

"such good or rare books as might seem necessary to the common library at Guildhall, for the profit of the students there, and those discoursing to the common people."

John Stow, writing of the Guildhall Chapel, gives the following account of this old Library and its destruction:

"Adioyning to this chapell on south side was sometimes a fayre and large librarie, furnished with bookes, pertaining to the Guildhall and colledge: these bookes (as it is said) were in the raigne of Edward the 6 sent for by Edward, Duke of Sommerset, Lord Protector, with promise to be restored shortly: men laded from thence three Carriers with them, but neuer returned. This librarie was builded by the executors of R. Whitington, and by William Burie: the arms of Whitington are placed on one side in the stone worke, and two letters, to wit, W and B for William Burie, on the other side: it is now lofted through, and made a store house for clothes."

From 1550 to 1824 is a long stretch, but it was not until the latter year that any steps were taken by the Corporation to re-establish their Library. The second founder was Mr. Richard Lambert Jones. On the 8th April, 1824, upon his motion, the Court of Common Council unanimously referred it to a Special Committee "to inquire and examine into the best mode of arranging and carrying into effect, in the Guildhall, a Library of all matters relating to this City, the Borough of Southwark, and the County of Middlesex, and to report thereon to this Court." Not long after—the Committee reported, recommending that the rooms then occupied by the Irish Society, in the east wing of the front of the Guildhall, should be adapted for the purposes of the new Library, and that meanwhile the front room by the Exchequer Court should be used as a temporary depository.

G

From this time the growth of the Library, though at first not rapid, has been steady and continuous, and marked at intervals by acquisitions of importance. In May, 1843, the autograph signature of Shakespeare, attached to the purchase-deed of a house in Blackfriars, dated 10th March, 1612, was bought at a sale in Messrs. Evans' rooms in Pall Mall for £145, and thus secured to the Library. In 1847, Mr. Philip Salomons presented to the Library a valuable collection of about 400 Hebrew books, for which the special thanks of the Court of Common Council were voted to him. A portion of the munificent bequest of £1,000 left in 1873 by his brother, Alderman Sir David Salomons, Bart., was applied to increasing the Hebrew Library and adding thereto a collection of works illustrating the history and present condition of the Jews throughout the world.

The time at length came when the Guildhall Library was to be provided with a home more suitable to its needs and importance, and more favourable to its future growth. In 1869, the Court of Common Council resolved to erect a new Library and Museum. The total cost exceeded £100,000. The yearly attendance of readers and visitors rose at once from 14,316 in 1868, the last year of the old Library, to 173,559 in 1874, the first complete year of the new. The lapse of twenty-five years since the opening of the new Library—years of great progress in all respects—has severely taxed the capacity even of the present building. The total number of visitors in 1897 was 414,977, of whom 76,004 were readers in the Library, 143,471 in the Newspaper Room, and 195,502 visitors to the Museum. The number of books at the last enumeration amounted to over 112,000 volumes, besides 32,000 pamphlets. The annual cost of maintenance is over £5,000, inclusive of £1,000 per annum granted for the purchase of books.

The Library is particularly rich in the following subjects: The history and topography of London and Middlesex; British topography including histories of counties, cities, towns, and parishes; publications of literary, scientific and archæological societies; genealogical and heraldic works, including parish registers, heralds' visitations and pedigrees; British history and biography; English poetry; Dictionaries and grammars of foreign languages; Archæology; Architecture and costume; Technical and scientific works; manuscripts and early printed books.

In the course of this brief sketch, it has been abundantly shown with what anxious care the Corporation and its Library Committee have laboured to make the Guildhall Library worthy of its name, and as useful as possible to the public at large. It is worthy of note that this Library was the pioneer of the Free Library movement; for many years there has been no restriction to the admittance of the public.

THE LIBRARY AND MUSEUM

lie at the east end of the Guildhall and occupy the site of some old and dilapidated houses formerly fronting Basinghall Street and extending back to the Guildhall. The total frontage of the new buildings to this street is 150 feet, and the depth upwards of 100 feet. The structure consists mainly of two rooms or halls, placed one over the other, with newspaper, committee and muniment rooms surrounding them. Of these two halls, the Museum occupies the lower site. The entrance to the building is by a Porch, having wrought iron entrance-gates, in Basinghall Street. The building was erected in 1873 from the designs, and under the superintendence, of the late Sir Horace Jones, the Architect of the Corporation. The style of architecture is perpendicular Gothic, in accordance with that of the Guildhall. The following is an architectural description :—

The principal Library is 100 feet long, 65 feet wide and 50 feet in height, divided into nave and aisles; the latter

Photo. by the Sandell Plate Co., Ld.

THE PRINCIPAL LIBRARY.

form twelve bays, fitted with oak book cases. This room is well lighted, the clerestory over arcade of the nave, with the large windows at the north and south ends together with those in the aisles, transmitting a flood of light to every corner of the room. The beautiful roof comprises arched ribs, which are supported by the Arms of the twelve great City Companies, with the addition of those of the Leather-sellers' and Broderers', and also the Royal and City Arms. The timbers are richly moulded, and the spandrels filled in with tracery. There are three large louvres for lighting the roof and providing ventilation. The aisle roofs, the timbers of which are also richly wrought, have louvres over each bay, and at night are lighted by means of sun-burners suspended from each of these louvres, together with those of the nave (electric light is now supplied throughout the whole building). Each spandrel of the arcade has, next the nave, a sculptured head, representing History; Poetry; Print-ing; Architecture; Sculpture; Painting; Philosophy; Law; Medicine; Music; Astronomy; Geography; Natural History, and Botany. The several personages chosen to illustrate these subjects being Stow, Camden; Shakespeare, Milton; Guten-berg, Caxton; William of Wykeham, Christopher Wren; Michael Angelo, Flaxman; Holbein, Hogarth; Bacon, Locke; Coke, Blackstone; Harvey, Sydenham; Purcell, Handel; Galileo, Newton; Columbus, Raleigh; Linnæus, Cuvier; Ray, and Gerard. There are three fireplaces in this room. The one at the north end, executed in D'Aubigny stone, is very elaborate in detail, the frieze consisting of a panel of painted tiles, the subject being an architectonic design of a procession of the Arts and Sciences, with the City of London in the centre, emblematised by an enlarged representation of the ancient seal, and some mediæval buildings with a river in the foreground. The quatre-foil panels on either side have sculptured heads of Carpenter, the founder of the City of London School, and of Chaucer, the 'Father of English

Poetry.' The two chimney pieces at the south end are also carved and foliated with the words " Anno Domini MDCCCLXXII." on the frieze of one, and " Domine Dirige Nos," the City motto, on the other, surmounted in both instances with the Royal, City, Middlesex, Westminster, and Southwark shields of Arms. The screens in front of these fireplaces are executed in oak, the panels being inlaid with coloured foreign woods, and the bases of the screens forming dwarf bookcases, which are fitted to receive large folio books.

On State occasions the Lord Mayor receives the distinguished guests in this room, which, from its spaciousness and light appearance, enhances the brilliancy of such assemblages.

THE STAINED GLASS WINDOWS.

Considering the purpose of the building, the stained glass in it required a special treatment, so as to admit as much light as possible, consistent with a decorative effect ; consequently a large amount of white glass has been introduced and the colour concentrated.

The large North Window of seven lights, divided by a transom, is the gift of some of the inhabitants of the Ward of Aldersgate. It has two major subjects, or pictures, in rich colours, and eight single figures.

The subject, occupying the three upper centre lights, is the Introduction of Printing into England, and represents Caxton and his Printing Press in the Almonry at Westminster ; the principal or centre figure being the great Printer showing to King Edward the Fourth and the Abbot of Westminster his works. Wynkyn de Worde is engaged at the Press, pulling a proof ; Pynson is carrying a forme ; in the background a boy is engaged mulling the ink. The four side figures are Gutenberg, who was the first to conceive the idea of printing from

movable types ; Wynkyn de Worde, foreman to Caxton ;
Pynson, one of his workmen, who succeeded him in his
business, and subsequently became the king's printer ; and
Bishop Coverdale, the translator of the Bible. The
treatment of these figures is what is termed grisaille,
so as to complement the colours in the centre group.
The subject in the three lower centre lights is Richard de
Bury, Bishop of Durham, purchasing the Library of the Abbot

THE NORTH WINDOW.

of St. Alban's for fifty pounds' weight of silver. This, also, is
in rich colours, and the four side figures, like the upper ones,
are in grisaille, on a silver quarry ground. The figures
represent Whitington and Gresham, both founders of libraries
in this City, Stow, the first city historian, and Milton. Below is
a representation of the old Aldersgate.

The Clerestory contains twenty-eight windows, having two lights each, in which are represented the symbols of the Planets, also Night and Day, upon a grisaille quarry ground. The aisles are lighted by fourteen windows of three lights each, having the Signs of the Zodiac, also on quarry grounds, with labels running across, containing short sentences from the works of Shakespeare.

The South Window contains the armorial bearings of several of the minor Livery Companies, by whom the window was presented. The window contains seven lights, and tracery consisting of the Royal Badges and some conventional ornaments. Each light contains the Arms of three Companies, the Arms being placed in the following order :—

> First Row.—Dyers, Brewers, Leathersellers, Pewterers, Barbers, Cutlers, and Bakers.

> Second Row. — Wax-chandlers, Tallow-chandlers, Armourers and Braziers, Girdlers, Butchers, Saddlers and Carpenters.

> Third Row.—Cordwainers, Founders, Broderers, Coopers, Joiners, Cooks, and Stationers.

Adjoining the Library, on the east side, is the Committee Room, which is lighted by windows looking on to Basinghall Street, and has a very richly moulded waggon-headed roof, the principal ribs of which are supported on stone corbels, bearing the shields of Arms of the several members of the Committee specially appointed for the erection of this building. The windows in this room are filled with glass in hexagonal quarries, each having a varied object of animal, bird, or flowers, and medallions representing the four Seasons, the Elements, Printing, Engraving, Time, &c. In the centre window are the Arms of Sir Sills John Gibbons, Bart., Sir Thomas Dakin, and Robert Besley, Esq., during whose mayoralties the building was erected.

THE NEWSPAPER AND PERIODICAL ROOM.

At the south end of the Library, is a commodious apartment, 50 feet in length by 24 feet wide, lighted by a stained glass window at the west end, and also by sky-lights in the roof. The subject of the window is the "School of Philosophy," taken from Raphael's celebrated mural painting; the principal personages represented are Plato, Aristotle, Archimedes, Socrates, Zoroaster, Alcibiades and Pythagoras. It was presented by Baron Lionel de Rothschild, then one of the Members of Parliament for the City of London.

IN THE VESTIBULE OF THE LIBRARY

is to be seen a very fine and unique collection of gold and silver medals and badges, seals and other official insignia of the Livery Companies of the City of London, including reproductions of the Master's badge of several of the Companies. Some of these are of the 18th century. The greater part have been presented to the Museum by the respective Companies. There is also a chronological series of badges worn by members of Committees conducting public receptions and entertainments given by the Corporation; historical City medals in gold, silver, and bronze, of the 16th-19th centuries; medals struck by the Corporation of the City of London to commemorate Civic events; medals struck in honour of printers and printing (Blades' Collection); and a complete series of medals struck by the Governments of France (Paris), Belgium and the Netherlands, and presented to the Corporation of London.

There are four cases containing Egyptian, Etruscan, Greek, and Roman Antiquities which demand special attention. These contain vestiges of "vanished æons," as Carlyle has it, and consist of engraved gems, jewellery, coins, medals, terra cottas, vases, glass, &c. The case of medals of the 15th to 18th century contains many very fine examples of the medallic art of the period. This collection is lent to the Corporation by William Rome, Esq., F.S.A., a member of the Common Council and "Chief Commoner," 1899.

Passing from the vestibule, there is in the east lobby a valuable collection of watches and watch and clock-work, which, by agreement with the Worshipful Company of Clockmakers, has been deposited there for public inspection. The collection clearly illustrates the progress of the art of watch-making from its commencement. The collection embraces numerous specimens of the works of the most celebrated makers of past times in clock, chronometer and watch work. Amongst these may be mentioned the celebrated John Harrison, the "Father of Chronometry" as he has been called, one of whose earliest productions, a wooden long clock, and his latest achievement, the duplicate of the chronometer which secured for him the reward of £20,000 offered by Government in accordance with the Act of Parliament of the 12th Queen Anne, 1714, are to be found, whilst examples of the highest interest of the works of Edward East, Tompion, Graham, Mudge, Daniel Quare, Larkham Kendall, Langley Bradley, Ellicott, the Arnolds, the Brockbanks, Vulliamy, the Frodshams and others are also included. The specimens are remarkable in respect to the movements, as evidencing the progress of the horological art, and for their workmanship, and as regards the cases, for their artistic excellence. Many of these specimens were presented to the Company by the Rev. H. L. Nelthropp, M.A., F.S.A. Master (1893 and 1894). A fine collection of Roman, Venetian and Florentine mosaics, chiefly of the 17th and 18th centuries, and of artistic snuff-boxes, &c., belonging to the same gentleman is also exhibited on loan.

Passing from here down the handsome stone staircase, we notice three finely sculptured stone statues. These were executed in the early part of the seventeenth century, and erected in the front of the old Chapel in Guildhall Yard. Much uncertainty exists as to the persons they are supposed to represent, but there is good reason to believe that the male figures are Edward VI. and Charles I. ; but there is greater divergence of opinion as to the female figure. On the whole, the probability is that it represents Henrietta Maria, the consort of Charles I. Old prints and copies of illuminated addresses presented to distinguished personages, adorn the walls. The stained glass window on the staircase is worthy of attention. It contains the arms of the following Companies :—Painters, Plumbers, Poulters, Tylers and Bricklayers, Scriveners, Turners, Loriners, Bowyers, Spectacle Makers, Wheelwrights, Masons, Coach and Coach Harness Makers, Glass Sellers, Clockmakers, and Plasterers. In a case underneath are specimens of ancient and artistic binding, miniature books, quaintly illustrated works, and other literary curiosities.

At the bottom of the staircase on the right is the entrance from Basinghall Street, and on the left, after descending a broad staircase, we find ourselves in the Museum, the floor of which is level with the ancient Crypt of the Guildhall, with which it directly communicates, and is consequently somewhat below the present level of Basinghall Street. This room, divided into nave and aisles, is 83 feet long and 64 feet wide, and has a clear height of 20 feet. It thus forms an imposing receptacle for the Archæological treasures of the City. The large fire-proof muniment rooms on this floor hold some of the valuable archives of the City.

The Museum.

THIS collection of antiquities is almost entirely composed of 'finds' within the City walls, and comprises objects discovered during the excavations for New London Bridge approaches, the Post Office, and the Royal Exchange, 1825-40, and in later years from excavations, often of great depth, for public and other buildings and for underground railways.

One of the most striking objects is the superb Roman mosaic pavement, 20 feet long and 13 feet 6 inches wide, found in Bucklersbury (close to the Mansion House) at a depth of 19 feet below the present surface. It is in an almost perfect state of preservation. There are also examples of mosaic pavements found in Cheapside, Leadenhall Street, and other places, besides many other interesting relics of the Roman occupation, such as memorial statues, monuments, pottery, lamps, needles, bronzes, &c.

The Museum is very rich in relics of mediæval times, and contains specimens of pottery, bronzes, armour, swords and daggers of various kinds, and leather work, including a series of shoes, illustrative of the changes of fashion in different periods. In addition to the many exhibits valuable to the antiquarian student, there are others that will be found interesting to the general visitor, such as the sword of the French commander at the Battle of the Nile, presented to the City, in a characteristic letter by Nelson, which is also shown ; several autograph letters of other public men, Wellington, Garibaldi, Palmerston ;

autographs of Shakespeare, Wren, Queen Elizabeth, &c. There is a curious collection of old London signs, chiefly carved on stone, many of them as old as the rebuilding of the City after the Great Fire. Space will not permit of mention of more than a few of the most striking — the 'Boar's Head' from Eastcheap (Falstaff's trysting-place) ; the 'Three Crowns' from Lambeth Hill ; 'George and the Dragon' from George Yard ; the 'Cock and Bottle' from Cannon Street ; a 'Dolphin' from the old Royal Exchange ; the 'Goose and Gridiron' from St. Paul's Churchyard ; and two versions of the 'Bull and Mouth' from St. Martin's-le-Grand. The larger one of these was placed over the front entrance of one of the most famous of the old coaching inns—the Bull and Mouth, a corruption of 'Boulogne Mouth' or Boulogne Harbour. A statuette of a bull appears within a large open mouth, on either side are bunches of grapes, above, the arms of Christ's Hospital on whose ground the inn stood, while a bust of Edward VI. surmounts the whole. On the lower portion is a tablet containing the following doggerel couplet :—

"Milo the Cretonian an ox slew with his fist,
And ate it up at one meal—ye gods ! what a glorious twist ! "

The other version was placed over the back entrance in Angel Street to the inn yard, and consists of a bull, nearly half life-size, standing over an immense gaping mouth. Other interesting exhibits are a fireplace from an old mansion in Lime Street, and a wooden figure of Time with scythe and hour-glass from the Church of St. Giles, Cripplegate, probably carved by Saunders of Gog and Magog fame.

An illustrated catalogue of the collection is in course of preparation.

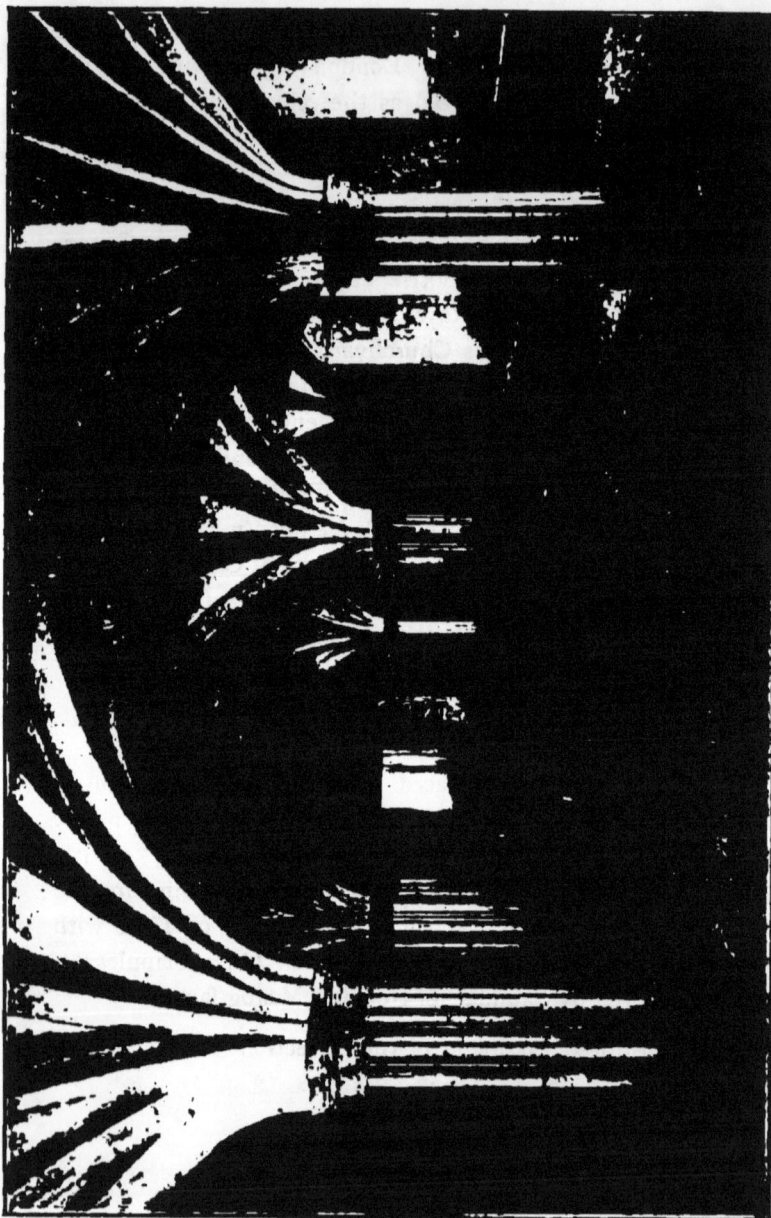

Photo. by the L. S. & P. C⁰., Ld.

THE EASTERN CRYPT.

Leaving the Museum, we pass into the

Eastern Crypt of the Guildhall.

THIS Crypt is of the same date as the Great Hall above it
(1411), and occupies rather more than half its basement. It
is considered to be the finest and most extensive under-crypt in
London. The dimensions are 77 feet by 46 feet, the height from
the ground to the crown of the arches 13 feet. It is remarkable
both for the elegance of its design and the perfect condition of
nearly all its members. It is divided into equal bays—four from
east to west and three from north to south—by six clustered
pillars, each composed of four half columns connected by fillets
and hollow mouldings ; the responds to the walls are half
pillars, those in the angles quarter pillars ; the shafts are of
Purbeck marble, the caps, bases, and vaulting ribs of firestone,
the spandrils of the vaults of chalk, the walls of rough
coursed work.

At the intersections and points of the ribs an interesting
series of carved bosses, 10 inches diameter, is introduced.
Those in the centre of the groins being large roses, 21 inches
diameter, bearing shields which are charged with the arms
assigned to King Edward the Confessor, viz. :—*azure* a cross
flory between five martlets *or* ; the large shield rose on the
vaulting of the north-east bay is charged with crossed
swords ; this is the arms of the See of London, which are
gules, two swords in saltire *argent*, hilted and pommelled
or, the origin of the objects selected is to typify the swords

of both St. Peter and St. Paul. The remaining two shields have the Arms of England and Russia emblazoned upon them, and are modern. The City Arms are in the side aisle, and those of St. George in the centre. In respect to the arms of the City of London, the illustration clearly shows that the object in the first quarter is a short Roman sword, in use in St. Paul's time, and is, in fact, intended, to be emblematical of St. Paul, the patron saint of the City. The association of the so-called 'dagger' with the City arms in connection with Walworth slaying Wat Tyler is altogether incorrect, notwithstanding the inscription underneath the statue of that famous Lord Mayor in Fishmongers' Hall. There is an historical City record which says "the new seal, upon which is a perfectly graven shield was brought in on the 17th April, 1381." Wat Tyler's death took place on 15th June in the same year. The sword was thus recognized in its proper place in the City Arms by Walworth himself, at least two months previous to his daring exploit. An early drawing at the "College of Arms" clearly shows that a sword, and not a dagger, is represented in the Arms. Some of the early deeds in connection with both the City and Bridge House Estates, bear the City Arms with an unmistakable Sword in the first quarter of the shield.

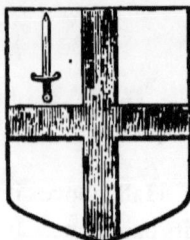

The north and south aisles originally possessed mullioned windows, which are now walled up ; at the western end is a bold and massive doorway, the opening is 11 feet high and 4 feet 8 inches in width : this leads to

The Western Crypt.

This is most probably the crypt of the ancient Guildhall, which Stow says extended towards Aldermanbury—it is now impossible to accurately determine the construction of this crypt, as probably the great fire of 1666 so damaged the vaulting that it was found desirable to remove it. The decline of Gothic architecture and the necessity for speedy reparation may account for the building of the brick walls and vaults which now fill the space and provide the bed for the pavement of the Hall above. There cannot, however, be any doubt but that the area of the crypt was vaulted, and that octagonal pillars 2 feet in diameter corresponding with the wall responds supported the ribs and groining, and consequently the floor of the Hall above, and that there were three aisles transversely. In the west wall, a window is visible at the end of both north and south aisles, and a doorway may be presumed to have occupied the centre.

Having now inspected the chief points of interest, the visitor should return through the Museum, into Basinghall Street, or through the Library into Guildhall Yard.

H

Officials, Ceremonies, &c.

THE survey of the Hall and of its various objects of interest being now completed, a short description of some of the sights witnessed nowadays therein, may be welcome. The annual election of Lord Mayor claims first attention, but before describing the ceremonies connected with the election, a short account of the office itself will be found interesting.

The Lord Mayor.

THE earliest mention of a Mayor in a formal document is said to occur in a writ of Henry II. The commonly received opinion, however, is that a change in the name of the Chief Magistrate of the City was made at the accession of Richard I. (1189). In a record preserved among the archives of the City it is stated: "In the same year (1 Richard I.), Henry Fitz-Eylwin, of Londenestane, was made Mayor of London, and was the first Mayor of the City, and continued to be such Mayor to the end of his life." In another document the "Mayor of London" appears in 1193 as one of the Treasurers appointed for Richard's ransom. In 1215, John granted to the citizens the right to elect, annually, their own Mayor.

The day of election of Mayor has been altered at various times. Formerly the election took place on the Feast of St. Simon and St. Jude (28th October). In 1346, it was changed to the Feast of the Translation of Edward the Confessor (13th October). Twenty years later, an order was made to revert to the old custom; but this order was soon ignored, and the election, until the year 1546, took place on the 13th October, when the election was ordered to take place thenceforth on Michaelmas Day. This date has remained unchanged to the present time.

Until 1376 the Mayor for the time being was elected by the Alderman and Sheriffs conjointly with the "whole commonalty." or with a deputation from the various Wards. In that year an ordinance was passed transferring the right of election to members selected by the rulers of the Guilds, their number varying according to the status of each Guild. This mode of election continued until 1384, when it was placed in the hands of the Common Council and "other men of the wards thereunto summoned." In 1467 the Guilds were again to the fore, the election being ordered to be made by the Common Council, the Master and Wardens of each mystery coming in their livery, and by "other good men specially summoned;" and the Livery continued to play an important part in each election until 1651, when an Act of Common Council again placed the right of election in the hands of the Aldermen, Common Council, and representatives of the Wards. Notwithstanding this Act, however, we find the Livery a few years later again exercising the right of election, and for a long time afterwards much friction continued to exist between the Guilds and the Wards, until the rights of the Livery were established by an Act of Pariament (ii. Geo. 1.)

Every Liveryman of any City Guild is now entitled to vote in Common Hall for Lord Mayor, Sheriffs, Chamberlain, Bridgemasters and a few minor officials.

It is especially to be noted that, before any Citizen of London can attain to the ancient and distinguished office of Lord Mayor, he must have been elected by a different body of electors on four distinct occasions :

First, by the rated inhabitants of the Ward he desires to represent as Alderman (this election being subject to the approval of the Court of Aldermen).

Second, by the Livery, in Common Hall assembled, on election as Sheriff (and then subject to the approval of the Sovereign).

Third, by the Livery, in Common Hall assembled to nominate two Aldermen for the office of Lord Mayor ; and

Fourth, by the Court of Aldermen, who finally select one of the two nominated to that office.

The Lord Mayor Elect is next presented to the Lord Chancellor for the approval, by the Sovereign, of the Citizens' choice. He, afterwards, namely on the 8th November, makes a statutory declaration at Guildhall, for the due execution of his office, and on the 9th November (Lord Mayor's Day) he goes in full state to the High Courts of Justice to make the due declaration before the Judges thereof.

The old Ceremonial Book makes the following observations on the office of Lord Mayor :—

" The Citizens have ever been jealous of the rights, privileges and powers with which the chief magistrate is invested, affecting as they do their property, liberty, and safety, that this office has been carefully restricted to the man of the public choice, that no one can occupy the civic chair until he has been three times subjected to popular election ; first, by the householders of the Ward he is elected to represent as Alderman, next, by the Liverymen as Sheriff, and thirdly, he is now eligible to be Lord Mayor and has to be nominated by the Liverymen, elected by the Aldermen, and approved by the Crown, subject, nevertheless, to the disqualification of bankruptcy or insolvency or otherwise. Thus secured from debasement, thus dignified with power, thus privileged and thus exalted is the chief magistrate of this great City by the choice of the people and the Sovereign's approval, and to this dignified position the son of the humblest citizen may aspire."

In the City, the Lord Mayor takes precedence of every subject of the Crown, including Princes of the Blood Royal. He is the head of the City Lieutenancy, and Admiral of the Port of London, and a Trustee of St. Paul's Cathedral. No troops may pass through the City without leave of the Lord Mayor first obtained, with the exception of the 3rd Battalion Grenadier Guards, the Royal Marines, and the Buffs (East Kent Regiment), each of whom are descendants of the Old Trained Bands, and have the right of marching through the City with fixed bayonets and colours flying. The password of the Tower is quarterly sent to him under the Sovereign's Sign Manual. He summons and presides over the several Courts and Meetings of the Corporation—the Court of Aldermen, the Court of Common Council, the

Court of Husting, and the Common Halls. They cannot be held but by his permission and direction, and the time of meeting, and the business to be placed on the Summons and discussed is entirely under his control. Nor can his presence be dispensed with, save by the appointment, in writing, under his hand and seal, of a *locum tenens*, who must be an Alderman who has passed the chair.

The Lord Mayor is the Chief Magistrate of the City, and a great part of his time is occupied in his duties as a Magistrate at his official residence, the Mansion House, where the Justice Room for the south part of the City is located. He is the first-named in the Commission of Oyer and Terminer, and General Gaol Delivery of the Central Criminal Court,—the principal Criminal Court in the Realm. He attends each session of that Court and hears and disposes of objections by persons summoned to serve upon the Grand Jury. He is one of the custodians of the City Seal. So numerous are the powers and duties of the Lord Mayor, that scarcely any civic function is performed independently of him.

Each Lord Mayor receives from the Corporation out of the City's cash the sum of £10,000 (in exchange for dues and other emoluments originally appertaining to the office) but so many and so great are the claims upon him, that he has to expend a much larger sum than this during his year of office. The Lord Mayor is looked upon as the dispenser of national hospitality, which for many years has almost exclusively devolved upon the Corporation of London. In all cases of public calamity—at home as well as abroad—the Lord Mayor of the day is the acknowledged Public Receiver and Almoner of Donations. Taking only the period comprised in the last twenty-five years, the Lord Mayor has raised no less a sum than £3,000,000, or an average of £120,000 a year, this includes the Hospital Sunday Fund, which amounts to about £40,000 annually. The amount collected in 1897 was a record one for charitable contributions, viz., £659,968 14s. 4d.

Election of a Lord Mayor.

THIS is still carried out with all the quaint and interesting ceremonies that have been observed for several centuries. In the first place, a precept from the Lord Mayor for the time being is addressed to the Masters and Wardens of the various Guilds to summon their Liverymen to the Guildhall, from thence to go to the Parish Church of St. Lawrence Jewry, there to hear divine service and a sermon, afterwards to return to Guildhall for the election of a Lord Mayor for the year ensuing. The Aldermen, Sheriffs and High Officers receive a summons to the same effect from the Swordbearer's office.

The first formal notice of this religious service is found in connection with the second election of Whitington. His first appointment to the Mayoralty was at the nomination of the King—his second, third and fourth, on his election by the citizens. On this occasion, solemn mass was said, a large body of the Livery attending the service in the "Guildhall Chapel" before proceeding to the election, and at "the unanimous entreaty of the Commoners to the Mayor and Aldermen, it was ordained that in every future year, the same religious ordinance should be observed, to the glory and praise of God and to the honour of the City." The service then first recorded, continues, though in a different form, to this day. The election of Mayor has always been preceded by divine service and a sermon, either in the Chapel formerly attached to the Guildhall, or, as now, in the "fair Church of St. Lawrence, called in the Jewry, because of old time many Jews inhabited thereabouts."

The Lord Mayor and Sheriffs go from the Mansion House in full state, and on arrival at Guildhall are received by the Aldermen and officers in the Aldermen's room. The Lord Mayor, Aldermen, Recorder, and Sheriffs are in black court suits and scarlet gowns ; the Lord Mayor and the Aldermen who have passed the chair wear their hoods and chains ; the Aldermen next in turn for the chair being in full dress, with lace frill ; the officers in full dress, with their gowns. A nosegay is presented to each by the Hallkeeper. The whole (conducted by the City Marshal), walk in procession from Guildhall to St. Lawrence's Church, in the following order :

Sheriffs' Chaplains, Under Sheriffs, High Bailiff of Southwark, Surveyor, Secondary, City Solicitor, Remembrancer, Comptroller, Judge of the City of London Court, Common Serjeant, Town Clerk, Chamberlain, Sheriffs, Aldermen below the chair (juniors first), Recorder, Aldermen above the chair (juniors first), City Marshal, Chaplain, Common Crier, Sword-bearer, The Lord Mayor.

The Aldermen, Sheriffs, and officers divide on each side of the aisle in the church, to allow the Lord Mayor to pass to his proper seat ; each afterwards following in turn to his own seat.

The Communion service only is said, and a sermon preached by the Lord Mayor's chaplain. The Lord Mayor, Aldermen, Sheriffs, and officers return from the church, in the same order in which they went, into the Aldermen's room ; and afterwards go down into the Great Hall, and take their seats on the Hustings—which is erected at the east end of the hall, and strewn with sweet smelling herbs, a relic of the times when London was not so sanitary as at present, and when the pungent smell of the herbs served to overpower the less pleasant odours around—the Recorder and the Aldermen who have passed the chair on the right of the Lord Mayor, and the

Aldermen who have not passed the chair on his left. After the Lord Mayor, Aldermen, Sheriffs, and officers are seated, the Common Crier proclaims silence, and directs all persons to be uncovered, and those who are not Liverymen to depart the hall on pain of imprisonment. The Common hall is opened by the Common Crier repeating the following proclamation—"Oyez, Oyez, Oyez! You good men of the Livery of the several Companies of this City, summoned to appear here this day for the election of a fit and able person to be Lord Mayor of this City, for the year ensuing, draw near and give your attendance."

After which the Recorder (or in his absence the Common Serjeant) rises from his seat, and, having first made his obeisance to the Lord Mayor, goes to the front of the Hustings and there makes his obeisance to the Livery. He then informs the Livery of the occasion of their meeting, and states that, in order that the choice of the Livery may be unfettered, the Lord Mayor and his brethren, the Aldermen, who have passed the chair, will retire. The Lord Mayor, Aldermen, and Recorder, then retire to the Aldermen's room, preceded by the Marshal and Swordbearer, the door being closed and kept by the Marshal,—the Common Crier remaining in the hall.

The Sheriffs, with the Common Serjeant between them, advance to the front of the Hustings, when the Common Serjeant reads to the Livery a list of the names of those Aldermen below the chair, who have served the office of the shrievalty (which has been previously furnished to him by the Town Clerk), and informs them that out of the Aldermen named they are to return two to the Lord Mayor and Aldermen, for them to choose which of the two shall be Lord Mayor for the year ensuing. They then proceed to the election, the Common Crier repeating after the Common Serjeant in this manner :—"So many of you as will have

A. B., Esq., Alderman, and ——— to be Lord Mayor of this City for the year ensuing, hold up your hands." And so through the list of those Aldermen below the chair who have been Sheriffs ; the name of each Alderman, as it is proposed, being exhibited on a board.

The Common Serjeant next, by direction of the Sheriffs, declares to the Livery that the Sheriffs are of opinion that their election has fallen upon A. B., Esq., Alderman, and ——— and C. D., Esq., Alderman and ——— [the candidate's Company].

If no poll be demanded (or when the poll is finished and the election declared), the two Sheriffs with the Common Serjeant between them, and the other officers, preceded by the Junior Aldermen and the Common Crier with his mace on his shoulder, proceed to the Aldermen's room, where the Lord Mayor and the Senior Aldermen are sitting, the Lord Mayor being covered. On entering, the Sheriffs and Common Serjeant make three obeisances to the Court ; the first at the entrance, the second in the middle of the court, and the third at the table ; the Lord Mayor acknowledging each, and at the third taking off his hat. Thirteen Aldermen in all must be present at the election.

The Common Serjeant at the table, between the Sheriffs, and attended by the other officers, reports the names of the persons on whom the election has fallen. The Recorder, Common Serjeant, and Town Clerk then go down to the table at the further end of the court to take the scrutiny, the Town Clerk writing the names of the two Aldermen returned by the Livery ; and each Alderman present, beginning with the junior, comes down to the table and declares to the Town Clerk for which of the two he votes, the Recorder and Common Serjeant overlooking to see that no mistake is made in scoring. The Recorder then goes up to his seat in court on the right hand of the Lord Mayor, the Common Serjeant

Photo by the L. S. & P. Co. Ld.

A COMMON HALL.   ELECTION OF LORD MAYOR.—THE OUTGOING LORD MAYOR RETURNING THANKS, 1897.

also goes to his seat, and the Town Clerk goes up to the Lord Mayor to know for which of the two Aldermen his lordship votes. Both the Recorder and Common Serjeant are to hear his lordship's vote, and see it marked. The result of the election is then declared by the Recorder.

The Swordbearer (in white gloves) hands the Lord Mayor Elect to his place, which is on the left hand of the Lord Mayor. The Lord Mayor Elect then addresses the Court of Aldermen, thanking the Court for the honour done him, and requesting their aid and assistance in the execution of his office. The Aldermen present, according to seniority, come up and congratulate the Lord Mayor Elect on his election: the officers do the like. The Lord Mayor, Aldermen, Sheriffs, and officers then go down to the great Hall, the Lord Mayor Elect being on the left hand of the Lord Mayor. The Recorder declares the election to the Livery.

The Lord Mayor Elect is called upon by the Town Clerk to declare his assent to take upon himself the office; after which the Swordbearer places the chain upon the Lord Mayor Elect, who makes a speech to the Common Hall. At this point in the proceedings, the Lord Mayor and Sheriffs are thanked by the Livery for their services, and only on very rare occasions has a proposed vote of thanks been refused.

The Common Hall is then dissolved, the Common Crier repeating from the Town Clerk as follows:—"You good men of the Livery of the several Companies of this City, summoned to appear here this day for the election of a Lord Mayor of this City for the year ensuing, may depart hence at this time, and give your attendance here again upon a new summons." The Lord Mayor takes the Lord Mayor Elect to the Mansion House in his state coach, the Lord Mayor Elect sitting on the left-hand side of the Lord Mayor. They are attended by the Aldermen, Sheriffs, and officers.

An Alderman who has been elected by the Livery, and who refuses to serve the office of Lord Mayor, is liable to a fine of £1,000.

The "Swearing in"

IS, probably, the most interesting ceremony in connection with the Lord Mayor Elect. This takes place the day previous to Lord Mayor's Day, when the Lord Mayor Elect takes upon himself the office of Mayor, although, until he has made his declaration before the Judges on November 9th, he has no power to act in any matter appertaining to his office. The Lord Mayor, accompanied by the Aldermen, Sheriffs, Officers, and the Lord Mayor's ' Company,' leaves the Mansion House from the front entrance, for Guildhall, in his private state carriage and four horses, attended by the Swordbearer, Common Crier, and Chaplain. Afterwards the Lord Mayor Elect, in his private state carriage, attended by his Chaplain and his own ' Company,' proceeds from the side entrance of the Mansion House to the Guildhall. The Lord Mayor, Aldermen, and Officers go into the Aldermen's room, where they await the arrival of the Lord Mayor Elect, who is introduced by two Aldermen who have passed the Chair. The Companies of the Lord Mayor and the Lord Mayor Elect go to the Hustings, and stand on each side in waiting, while a Court of Aldermen is held, at which the Lord Mayor takes leave of the Court. The procession then goes from the Aldermen's room to the Great Hall. After the Lord Mayor, Aldermen, Recorder, Sheriffs, and High Officers have taken their seats on the Hustings, the Common Crier with the Mace upon his shoulder walks up to the table, making three low reverences, and stands at the table with the Mace

placed before him on the floor. The Town Clerk, standing
on the north side of the table, makes a low reverence, and
afterwards two others. The Town Clerk, standing at the side
of the table, then administers the Declaration to the Lord
Mayor Elect, who stands on the opposite side of the table.
Then the Lord Mayor Elect makes and subscribes the
Declaration (I . . . do solemnly, sincerely, and truly declare
that I will faithfully perform the duties of my Office of Mayor
of the City of London) required by the 12 sect. of 31 and 32
Vic., cap. 72, on which the *late* Lord Mayor surrenders his seat
to the *new* Lord Mayor, and takes his seat on the left side.

The Chamberlain, making three reverences, walks to the
south side of the table and presents the diamond Sceptre to
the late Lord Mayor, by whom it is delivered to the new Lord
Mayor, who places it upon the table before him. The Chamberlain then retires, making three reverences ; and advancing again
in the same manner as before, presents the Seal of the office of
Mayoralty, which being disposed of on the table as before, he
retires ; then, advancing a third time, he presents in the same
manner the Purse, which is also placed on the table, and the
Chamberlain then retires. The Swordbearer next advances
with three reverences, and presents the Sword to the late
Lord Mayor, by whom it is given to the new Lord Mayor,
who delivers it again to the Swordbearer, who places it on
the table and retires, making three reverences. The Common
Crier then advances with three reverences, and presents the
Mace to the late Lord Mayor, by whom it is given to
the new Lord Mayor, who delivers it to the Common Crier ;
he lays it upon the table and retires, making three reverences.
The Chamberlain's Chief Clerk advances, making three reverences, and receives from the Lord Mayor, on a velvet cushion,
the Sceptre, the Seal, and the Purse, and retires. The Swordbearer then advances, making three reverences, and takes the
Sword from the table and retires, making three bows. The

Common Crier takes the Mace with the same ceremonies. The Aldermen, Sheriffs, and High Officers, in rotation, advance to the Lord Mayor and congratulate him. The Remembrancer then presents to the Lord Mayor a deputation for the City Gauger, which his Lordship signs. The Comptroller presents the Indenture for the City Plate, which the Lord Mayor signs. The late Lord Mayor then delivers up the key of the City Seal to the new Lord Mayor.

The following is the old order of administering and the form of the

Lord Mayor's Oath.

The Town Clerk, kneeling down on a stool at the side of the table, then administers the following oath to the Lord Mayor Elect, who stands on the opposite side of the table :—

"Ye shall sweare that ye shall well and lawfully serue the Queen's Maiesty in the office of Maioralty in the Citty of London ; and the same Citty ye shall surely and safely keepe, to the behoofe of her highnes, her heires, and lawfull successors ; and the profitt of the Queen yee shall doe in all things that to you belongeth ; and the right of the Queen, that to the crown appertayneth, in the same Citty of London lawfully ye shall keepe. Ye shall not consent to the decrease ne concealement of the rights ne of the franchises of the Queen ; and wheresoever ye shall knowe the rights of the Queen or of the crowne (be it in lands or in rents, fraunchises or sutes) concealed or withdrawn, to your power ye shall doe to repeale it : and if ye may not ; ye shall say it to the Queen, or to them of her counsell that ye wete will say it to the Queen. Also lawfully and rightfully ye shall entreate the people of your Balliewick ; and right shall ye doe to every one, as well to strangers as others, to poore as to riche, in that that belongeth you to doe : and that for highnes ne for ryches, for gyfte ne for behest, for favour ne for hate, wrong shall ye doe to no man : ne nothing shall ye take by the which the Queen should leese or right be disturbed or letted. And good assize shall ye set upon bread, wyne, ale, fysh, flesh, corne, and all other victualls. Weights and measures in the same Citty ye shall doe to be kept, and due execution doe upon the defaults that thereof shall be founde, according to all the statuts thereof made, not repealed. And in all other things that to a mayor of the Citty of London belongeth to doe, well and lawfully ye shall doe and behaue you.

As God you helpe. ·

THE "SWEARING IN." INSIGNIA OF OFFICE DELIVERED TO THE LORD MAYOR, 1897.

Photo. by the L. S. & P. Co., Ltd.

The Lord Mayor's Insignia and Household.

THE Lord Mayor's collar is a handsome collar of SS., and is said to be one of the finest as well as the earliest of those known. It has formed part of the City's *Insignia* for over three-and-a-half centuries, having been bequeathed by Sir John Alen, a Citizen and Mercer, and sometime Alderman and Mayor of the City, who died in 1544, to the Lord Mayor for the time being and his successors, for use "uppon principall and festivall dayes." The collar was enlarged in 1567 by the addition of four S's., two knots and two roses. At the present day, it consists of twenty-eight richly-worked SS., with a Tudor rose and knot inserted alternately between the letters. The ends of the collar are joined by a port-cullis from which is suspended the jewel. The collar is made of gold throughout, and the Tudor roses, white upon red, are executed in enamel. It remained without a pendant until 1558, when Sir Martin Bowes, Citizen and Goldsmith, presented the City with a cross of gold with divers precious stones and pearls to be worn by successive Lord Mayors "at and with" the collar of SS. presented by Sir John Alen. This gift of Sir Martin Bowes has long since disappeared, nothing being known of its history subsequent to its disuse in 1607, when a new jewel was purchased by the City, which is substantially the same as that worn by Lord Mayors of the present day. It contains, in the centre, the full City arms, cut in cameo, of a delicate blue, on an olive ground. Surrounding this is a garter of bright blue, edged with white and gold, bearing the City motto, "Domine dirige nos," in gold letters. The whole is encircled with a wreath of eight roses, with the thistle and shamrock intertwined, composed of brilliants and rose diamonds set in silver. When worn without the collar, the jewel is suspended by a broad blue ribbon.

THE CITY SCEPTRE.

The ancient Mace, or, as it has long been called, the Sceptre of the City of London, is of an unique character. It measures a foot and a half in length, the shaft and knobs being of crystal, mounted in gold, and the head of gold, jewelled. The date of the Sceptre is unknown, and cannot be ascribed to any one period, for whilst the head appears to be of the 15th century, the shaft may very possibly date back to Saxon times. This Sceptre is carried by the Lord Mayor in discharging his office of chief butler at coronations.

THE SWORDBEARER AND THE CITY SWORDS.

The City Sword forms an important item of the Lord Mayor's *Insignia*, and there are indeed no less than four swords belonging to the City, viz. :—(1) The " Pearl " Sword, so-called from its scabbard being studded with pearls, and said to have been presented by Queen Elizabeth when she opened the first Royal Exchange in 1571—it bears the Solingen or Passau wolf-mark ; (2) the " Sword of State," the emblem of the Lord Mayor's authority—first used about 1680. The Sword of State is inverted with its point downwards in the presence of the Sovereign or any of the Judges—but is borne with the point upwards before the Lord Mayor on all other occasions of authority ; (3) the "Black" Sword, used on fast days in Lent and at the death of any of the Royal Family ; and lastly (4) the "Old Bailey Sword," which is placed above the Lord Mayor's chair when sitting at the

L

Central Criminal Court. It is probable that the "Black" Sword was first used in 1534, and the Old Bailey Sword in 1563. One of the earliest references in the City's archives to the City Swordbearer occurs in the *Liber Albus*, to the following effect, viz.: "Item, the Mayor shall have two other Sergeants (*i.e.*, besides the Common Crier) at least, and an Esquire, well bred (*bien nurry*) . . . to bear his sword before him." The fur cap, commonly spoken of as a "cap of maintenance" (although varying in shape from such caps as known in heraldry), and worn by the Swordbearer at the present day, forms a distinctive feature. When it took the modern shape it is difficult to say. We know that, in 1546, Sir Martin Bowes, the then Lord Mayor, presented the City with "a very

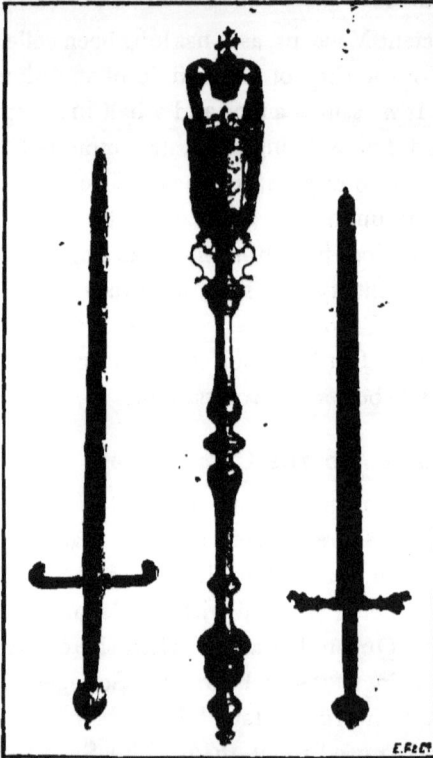

THE SWORD OF STATE   THE MACE.   THE PEARL SWORD.

goodly royale hatt," to be worn by the Swordbearer for the time being. His generosity in this direction may possibly have been stirred by the presentation of a sword in the previous year by Sir Ralph Warren, a late occupant of the Mayoralty chair. In those days it was customary for this officer to wear a silk or velvet hat in summer, and a fur cap in winter, but this custom has long fallen into disuse, and the only cap now worn is one of sable fur lined with black silk. His ordinary apparel, at the present day, comprises a gown of black brocaded satin of the same material as the Lord Mayor's State gown, but without the gold lace. On State occasions this is worn with a black Court suit, silk stockings, and shoes with silver buckles. The Cap of Maintenance is worn by the Swordbearer on all occasions, even in the presence of the Sovereign. The chief duty of the Swordbearer, besides his ceremonial duties, consists in warning the Lord Mayor, Aldermen, and Members of the Common Council to attend the various Courts and Meetings.

THE COMMON CRIER AND THE MACE.

The office of Common Crier is one of the most ancient of those attached to the Lord Mayor's household. As early as the 14th century we find him known as the Common Sergeant-at-Arms of the City, when he received a salary of sixty shillings a-year, besides his robes and certain fees, including one of twelve pence for every cry he made through the City. He was also provided with a horse " for the honour of the City." His full title in those days was "Sergeant Common Crier," and his chief duty then, as now, was to be ready at the commands of the Lord Mayor for the time being, " like other sergeants " of the same household.

At what period the City of London first employed a Mace or Maces is unknown, but there is evidence to show that, as early as 1252, there were Sergeants in the City who carried staves of some kind as emblems of authority, and that early in the 14th century there was an officer called the Mace Bearer, in the person of Robert Flambard. In 1354, the citizens obtained a Charter from the King, confirming what appears to have been a prescriptive right, enjoyed by the Sergeants-at-Mace of the City of London, to carry Silver Maces before the Mayor. The number of Sergeants-at-Mace attached to the Mayor and Sheriffs, each of them carrying a Mace, varied from time to time, but there seems to have been only one Mace borne before the Mayor. The earliest records contain no reference to this Mace, the first notice being in 1514, when the outgoing Mayor handed over to the new Mayor " the Mace for the Sergeaunt of Armes."

In 1559 a new Mace was made which was afterwards enlarged, and eventually stolen from the house of Lord Keeper Coventry. Another Mace was thereupon made, which served its purpose until 1649, when pursuant to an Order of Parliament, that all Maces of the Kingdom should conform to one pattern, the City bought a new one from the maker of the Parliamentary Mace. At the Restoration, this Mace gave place to one made by Sir Thomas Vyner, the well-known London Goldsmith, who had filled the Mayoralty Chair in 1653-4. Vyner's Mace continued to be used until 1735, when it was found to be past repair, and a new Mace was made— the Mace in use at the present day. This Mace is of silver gilt, of fine and elaborate workmanship. Its weight is 304 ounces, and length 5 feet 3 inches. The bowl of the head is divided by vertical bands into four compartments, in three of which are royal badges crowned, viz. : the fleur-de-lis, the rose and thistle united, and the harp, each of them accompanied by the letters $G^{II.}$ R., the initials of George II. In the fourth compartment are the City arms ; on the flat top of the head are the Royal arms. The head is surrounded by the usual circlet of crosses and fleurs-de-lis, from which spring the arches of the crown, surmounted by an orb and cross. Below the bowl are projecting arabesque figures ending in scrolls, and connecting it with the stem. The latter is of the baluster form, with several knops ; below the upper one is inscribed, " The Rt. Hon, Sir Edward Bellamy, Knt., Lord Mayor, 1735," and towards the lower end of the stem, " John Elderton, $Esq^{re.}$ Common Cryer and Sergeant-at-Armes, 1735." Other portions are inscribed with the dates of repairs and of re-gilding, with the names of the Lord Mayors at the time.

THE CITY MARSHAL.

The origin of this office is traceable to certain Letters Patent issued by Queen Elizabeth, in 1595, to Sir Thomas Wilfred, Provost Marshal in the City of London, with power to execute all such duties as were performed by Provost Marshals in counties. In this particular instance, the Provost Marshal's jurisdiction was not confined to the City, but extended over the adjacent counties of Middlesex, Surrey, Essex, and Kent, and his duties then, and for some time afterwards, were as much of a military as of a civil character. When, in course of time, his civil duties increased with the population, an additional Marshal was appointed to assist in keeping order in the streets of the City; the senior officer being known as the Provost or Upper Marshal, and his colleague as the Under Marshal. To them were committed the supervision of the Watch and Ward of the City, the ridding of the streets of all rogues and vagabonds, and the removal of the sick to the various hospitals. Each of them was provided with three assistants or marshalmen, and also with a horse. The passing of the several Police Acts of 1829 and 1839—the one introducing a new police system in the Metropolis and the other regulating the police in the City— left the City Marshals little beyond their ceremonial duties to perform, and when opportunity offered, their number was reduced to one.

THE MAYORALTY SEAL.

The original Mayoralty Seal is not in existence, having been destroyed in 1381, by order of the Civic Authorities as too small and not sufficiently handsome. The Seal which was then made to take its place, is the Mayoralty Seal now in use. It measures 2¼ inches in diameter. In its centre are seated figures of St. Peter (St. Thomas of Canterbury ?) and St. Paul. Above is a niche with the Virgin and Child, and in base a shield of the City Arms, supported by two lions. On each side of the central figures is a tall canopied niche containing a Sergeant-at-Arms, and above, a kneeling angel adoring the figure of the Virgin and Child. Legend : *Sigill : Maioratus : Civitatis : London.*

The Common Seal of the City.

The original Common Seal of the City dates from the early part of the 13th century. It was 2¾ inches in diameter and consisted of two matrices. The obverse bore (and still bears) a figure of St. Paul, the Patron Saint of the City, with a sword in his right hand, and in his left a banner of England. He is represented as standing in the middle of the City, and on either side are two great towers or castles. In front of all is the City Wall and Ditch, with gateway, in which is engraved a mullet or star. Legend : *Sigillum Baronum Londoniarum.* The reverse had in its base a view of the City surmounted by an arch, and on the top of the arch, seated on a throne or chair of state, a figure of St. Thomas à Becket, with figures kneeling on either side. At the Reformation, this reverse, after doing duty for three centuries, was broken up, and a new one made bearing the City Arms, in place of the figure of St. Thomas and his companions. The old obverse with the figure of St. Paul was fortunately left untouched, and with the new reverse of 1539, continues still to be the Common Seal of the City. The City Seal is only affixed in open Court, after formal Resolution. The Keys are different, and three in number, kept respectively by the Lord Mayor, the Chamberlain (as representing the Court of Aldermen), and the Comptroller or Vice-Chamberlain (as the representative of the Court of Common Council), and the Seal is only affixed to a document after the same has been examined and signed by one of the Law Officers of the Corporation.

Lord Mayor's Day

HAS been so often described that it is only necessary to state here that the whole of the arrangements of the 'Show' are in the hands of the Remembrancer and a body of sixteen gentlemen, known as the "Lord Mayor and Sheriffs' Committee"—half of whom are appointed by the Lord Mayor Elect, and the other half by the two Sheriffs—to them are entrusted the whole arrangements in gathering together and marshalling the Procession, and in issuing invitations to the Banquet in the evening. They act as Masters of the Ceremonies at the reception of guests by the Lord Mayor previous to the Banquet, and attend to the general comfort of the guests. The cost of the 'Show' and the Banquet usually amounts to about £4,000—half of which sum is defrayed by the Lord Mayor, and the other half by the Sheriffs.

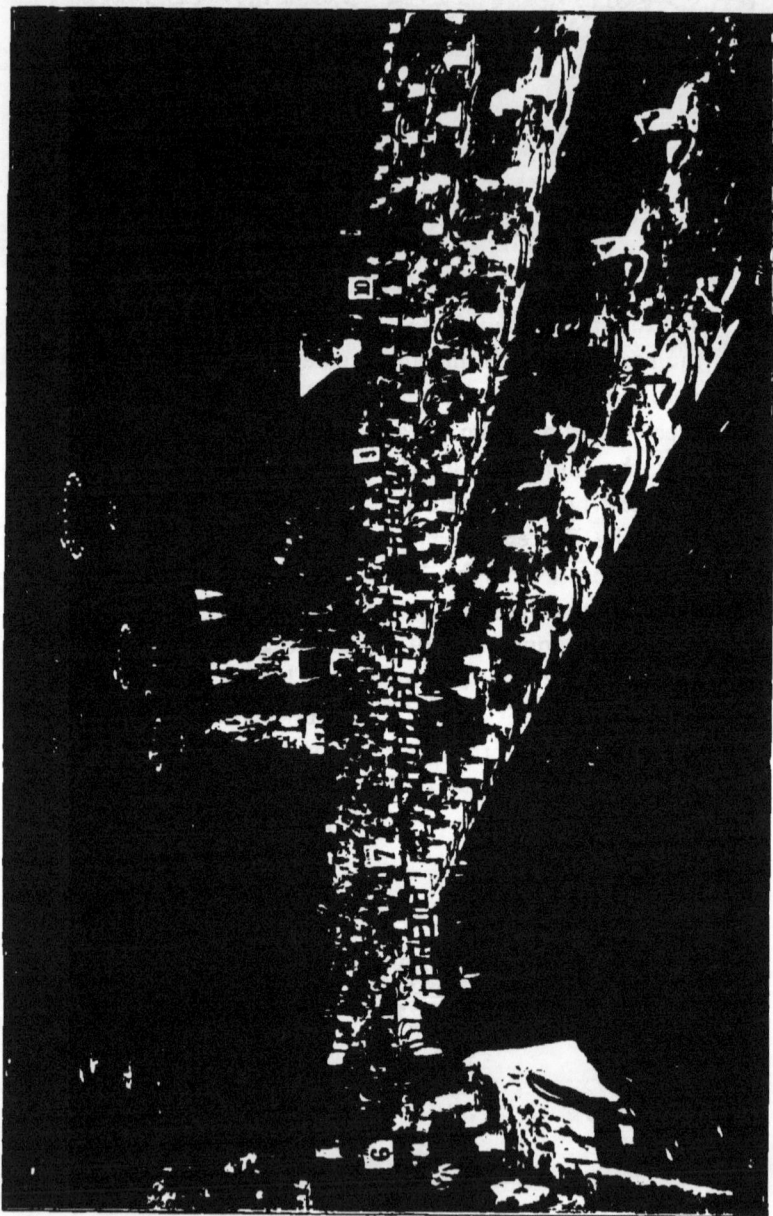

Photo. by the L. S. & P. Co., Ld.

THE TABLES LAID FOR THE LORD MAYOR'S BANQUET, 1897.

Lord Mayor's Banquet.

ON the night of the Banquet, the general body of guests assemble in a specially constructed crush room in Guildhall Yard, and pass through the corridor on the right to the Library, where they are received by the Lord Mayor and the Lady Mayoress. They then take their seats on either side of a roped off gangway, and await the arrival of the more important personages, the most distinguished of whom are met at the entrance of the Hall and conducted by the Reception Committee, preceded by the City Marshal and State Trumpeters, to the Lord Mayor, their names being announced by the Master of the Ceremonies ; the whole scene at this point is one of great brilliancy and splendour, the ladies' dresses and jewels, the military and other uniforms, the Judges' and the Aldermen's scarlet robes, and the mazarine gowns of the Common Councilmen make a magnificent spectacle.

The chief guests having all arrived, and been duly presented to the Lord Mayor, the general company move from the Library and take their allotted places at the tables in the Great Hall. Then, preceded by the City Marshal and the four State Trumpeters playing fanfares, and the Sword and Mace Bearers, come the Lord Mayor, (his train borne) with the chief lady guest on his arm, and the Lady Mayoress on the arm of the chief guest, usually the Prime Minister of the day (her train borne by a page, followed by six Maids of Honour, uniformly dressed who pass into the Drawing Room) ; then the late Lord Mayor, with his lady, led by a distinguished

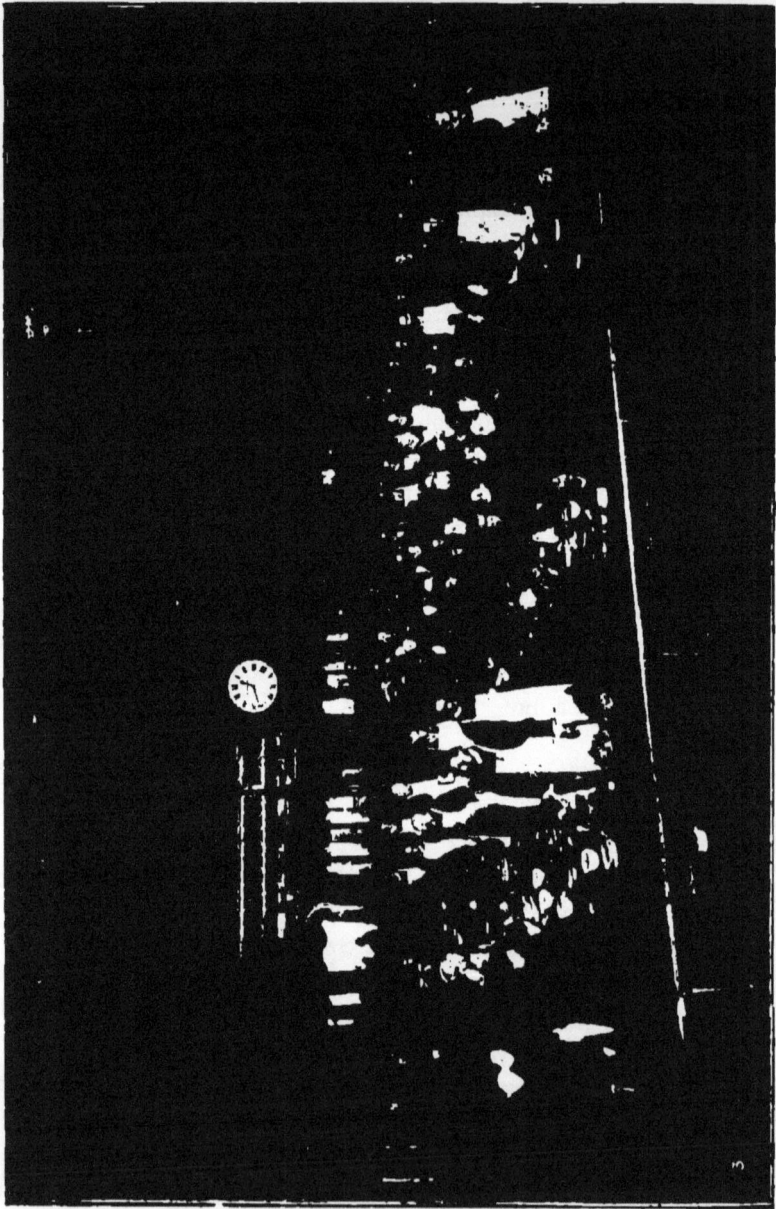

Photo. by the L. S. & P. Co., Ld.

DISTRIBUTION OF FOOD THE DAY AFTER THE LORD MAYOR'S BANQUET, 1897.

guest ; the Members of the Cabinet ; the Foreign Ambassadors ; Peers ; the Judges in their scarlet robes ; the Law Officers of the Crown ; and the Sheriffs, with their ladies.

The procession wends its way round the Hall to the seats set apart for the chief guests. Grace is duly said, before and after the dinner, by the Lord Mayor's Chaplain. The banquet over, the Lady Mayoress's Maids of Honour take their seats in a small gallery, specially erected in front of the principal table. The toastmaster announces the names of the most distinguished guests, and the loving-cup is circulated. The Loyal Toasts having been given by the Lord Mayor, are followed by one that always arouses the keenest interest—that of Her Majesty's Ministers.

In reply, the Prime Minister is expected to say something as to the past policy of Her Majesty's Government, and to announce their future intentions as to matters which, at the time, are specially interesting to the citizens of London or to the country at large. His speech is telegraphed from the Guildhall for transmission to all parts of the world. The illustration of the tables (on page 136) gives some idea as to the economy of space required to accommodate the 800 invited guests. On the right is seen a platform on which one of the barons of beef is carved ; beyond it, on the same side, is the elaborately-carved canopy, under which will be seated at the principal table the Lord Mayor and his chief guests, with the Sheriffs, one at each corner. On the shelves under the canopy is a brilliant display of Corporation Plate. The Sword and Mace of State are placed in the centre.

Liberal provision having been made for the needs of the guests, whatever is left unused is on the day following distributed among the poor. The illustration shows the members of the Lord Mayor and Sheriffs' Committee in readiness to make this distribution.

The Sheriffs.

THE Office of Sheriff of London appears to have existed very shortly after the Conquest. It is specifically mentioned in several of the early Charters granted to the citizens of London. Notwithstanding the removal, by the Local Government Act, 1888, of the right to elect a Sheriff of Middlesex out of the hands of the citizens of London, to whom it had been expressly granted by Charter of Henry I. (subsequently confirmed by John, Henry III., Edward I., and Edward III.), and for which they had ever since paid an annual rent, the City continues to elect two Sheriffs. Until the commencement of the 14th century, the Sheriffs were elected by the Mayor, Aldermen, and the "Good Men" of the City, or "Commonalty." In 1301, an attempt was made to restrict the number of electors to twelve representatives of each Ward, but this, like other subsequent attempts, proved unsuccessful. In 1347, is met with, for the first time, a new method of procedure. In that year, one of the Sheriffs was elected by the Mayor, and the other by the Commonalty, and this prerogative of the Mayor for the time being to elect one of the Sheriffs continued to be exercised with few, if any, exceptions, down to 1638. From 1642 to 1651, the Mayor's claim to elect a Sheriff was always contested. He might nominate, but not elect ; although, as a rule, the citizens paid him the compliment of electing his nominee to serve in conjunction with the Sheriff of their own choice. For the year 1652, and for some years afterwards, the Mayor neither nominated nor elected a Sheriff ; but, in 1662, when he would have elected one Bludworth as Sheriff, the Commonalty claimed their right, although they accepted the Mayor's nominee. For the next ten years (1663 to 1673) the Mayor's right of election passed unchallenged. In 1674, when objection was again raised, a Committee was appointed to enquire into the whole matter.

In its report is found a reference, made for the first time, to the custom of the Lord Mayor electing, or at least nominating, a Sheriff for the year ensuing, by drinking to him on some public occasion. This custom is said to have arisen in the reign of Elizabeth.

In 1878, by Act of Common Council, all Acts, Orders, and Ordinances regulating or enforcing the nomination or election to the Shrievalty being thereby repealed, it was declared (*inter alia*)—that the right of election to the office of Sheriff should vest in the Liverymen of the several Companies of the City, in Common Hall assembled, the 24th day of June in each year being fixed as the election day, and that casual vacancies be filled up by elections on days to be fixed by the Court of Aldermen. A fine of £200 was made payable by any person duly nominated, who should decline to take upon himself the office. And further, that between the 14th day of March and the 14th day of May in every year, the Lord Mayor should, in the Court of Aldermen, nominate one or more Freeman or Freemen of the City (not exceeding three in the whole) to be publicly put in nomination for the Shrievalty, to the Liverymen in Common Hall assembled, such nomination to remain in force for five years. In addition to persons thus nominated, every Alderman who has not served the office of Sheriff is, *ipso facto*, in nomination for the office, in priority to any other person, and it is competent for any two members of the Common Hall to nominate any Freeman of the City of London to the said office.

The absolute estate and interest in the office of Sheriff belong to the Corporation, which consequently retains the fees and emoluments of the office. An allowance of £750 is granted by the Corporation to the Sheriffs annually, they discharging thereout two Fee Farm Rents (£40 and £10 respectively), payable by the Corporation, and making their own arrangements with their Under-Sheriffs.

The duties of the Sheriffs of the City of London are multifarious, and, like those of the Lord Mayor, incessant. It is an especial privilege of the Sheriffs to wait upon the Sovereign, by direction of the Corporation, attended by the City Remembrancer, to ascertain the Royal will and pleasure as to the reception of Addresses from the Corporation. The duty and privilege of presenting, at the Bar of the House, Petitions to Parliament on behalf of the Corporation is discharged by the Sheriffs, attended by the City Remembrancer. They are required to attend every Session of the Central Criminal Court, and, of course, discharge the duties that ordinarily attach to their office.

They are expected to be in attendance on the Lord Mayor in the discharge of many of his official functions. They take charge of, and conduct, the business in the Common Hall, during the absence of the Lord Mayor. Places are reserved for the Sheriffs in the Courts of Aldermen and Common Council, which they usually occupy when not officially engaged elsewhere. The average cost to each gentleman serving the office may be put down at from £3,000 to £4,000.

A Sheriff wears a Chain of Office and Badge, which of late years has usually been presented to him by the inhabitants of the Ward or district with which he is associated. In connection with this it may be stated that the chain should be of the ordinary link pattern, and should not assume the character of a Collar of SS. The Collar of SS. is a very old emblem associated with the administration of justice, and worn as such by the Lord Chief Justice and other high judicial functionaries. The Lord Mayor alone, of the Aldermen, as Chief Magistrate of the City, is entitled to wear such a collar. The Badge should only shew designs specially appropriate to a Ward or district, or to the individual, and should not include the sword or mace, which do not appertain to the office of Sheriff.

Election and "Swearing In" of Sheriffs.

THE election of Sheriffs takes place on the Hustings, erected at the east end of the Guildhall, on Midsummer Day. On this day the Lord Mayor goes, in full state, from the Mansion House to the Guildhall. On arriving there, he proceeds to the Aldermen's room and, preceded by the Aldermen, Sheriffs and officers in the same order as at the election of Lord Mayor, from thence to the Hustings. The Common Hall is opened by the Common Crier, in the same form as in the election of a Lord Mayor, after which the Recorder, or in his absence the Common Serjeant, acquaints the Livery with the nature of the duty they are called upon to discharge, and then the Lord Mayor, Aldermen, and Recorder retire to the Common Council Chamber, where the Sword is placed on the table on a bed of roses. The Sheriffs, with the Common Serjeant between them, then advance to the front of the Hustings, when the Common Serjeant reads to the Livery a list of the persons to be put in nomination for Sheriffs, Chamberlain, Bridge-masters, Aleconners, and Auditors ; and the Sheriffs, assisted by the Common Serjeant and some of the City officers, proceed to the elections, which are determined by show of hands, unless a poll be demanded. When the elections are over, the Sheriffs, with the Common Serjeant between them, preceded by the Marshal and the Common Crier with the Mace on his shoulder, and followed by the City officers, proceed to the Council Chamber, where the Lord Mayor and the Court of Aldermen are sitting, the Lord Mayor being covered ; and, after making three reverences to the Lord

Mayor, each of which he acknowledges by taking off his hat, the Common Serjeant in the name of the Sheriffs reports the result of the elections.   The Lord Mayor, Aldermen, Recorder, Sheriffs, and officers *(if there be no poll)* proceed immediately to the Hustings in the Great Hall, when the Recorder declares to the Common Hall the persons elected, and the Common Crier calls upon the Sheriffs elect to come forth and declare their consent to take upon themselves their offices. The "swearing in" takes place on the 28th of September in the presence of the Lord Mayor, Aldermen, and the Courts of the Sheriffs' Companies, with the same officers in attendance as on the day of election.   When the Lord Mayor and Aldermen are seated on the Hustings, the Common Crier commands silence ;   and calls upon the Sheriffs Elect by name, to come forward and take upon themselves the office of Sheriff of London.   The Sheriffs Elect then come to the table, and the Town Clerk administers the declaration of office.   The Sheriffs then take off their gowns and put on violet gowns ; the Sheriffs retiring from office respectively taking off their own chains and gowns and putting the chains of office upon each of the new Sheriffs.

At this Common Hall the retiring Sheriffs usually receive the thanks of the Livery for their services.

A Sheriff, upon retiring from his office (unless he is an Alderman or a member of the Common Council) passes out of the public life of the Corporation.   If he desires to fill the office of Alderman, and pass in due course to the Mayoral Chair, he must be elected by the ratepayers of one of the twenty-five Wards, when a vacancy occurs by the death or resignation of its Alderman.   The mere fact of any person (other than an Alderman) having served the office of Sheriff is not (as is sometimes supposed) a stepping-stone to the office of Lord Mayor.

Principal Officers.

$\mathcal{A}$ SHORT account of the officers mentioned in the description of the foregoing Ceremonies may prove interesting.

THE RECORDER

holds the principal and most ancient office of any in the Corporation. He is the Senior Law Officer and the representative of the Lord Mayor and Aldermen in their judicial capacity. A record of his duties is preserved so far back as 1304. A few of his duties are here given. To advise the Lord Mayor and Aldermen for their better direction in administering law and justice. By custom and Charter, to record, testify, and declare the customs of London by word of mouth. To attend as one of the Judges of the Central Criminal Court, and to charge the Grand Jury. To sit as Judge in the Mayor's Court. To attend the Lord Mayor upon the presentation of Addresses from the Courts of Aldermen and Common Council to the Sovereign, and on all important public occasions. To attend the presentation of, and to present the Lord Mayor Elect to the Lord Chancellor, for the approval of the Sovereign, and to present the Lord Mayor to Her Majesty's Judges on his being sworn into office.

THE CHAMBERLAIN.

The office of the Chamberlain of London is one of great antiquity and responsibility. His office is mentioned in 1204. In 1278, Matthew de Columbers is mentioned as the Chamberlain of our Lord, the King. In 1300, the Chamberlain was elected by the Mayor and Aldermen. In 1319, it was ordered that he should be chosen by the

Commonalty and removed according to the will of the same. At the present time, he is elected annually by the Livery in Common Hall on Midsummer Day. In addition to his ceremonial duties, he has been, from time immemorial (and now is), the Treasurer or Banker of the City, and, in that capacity, has had the care and custody of the monies of the Corporation of London, called the City's Cash, and of the several funds committed to the management of the Corporation. The City's Cash Account for 1897 is the 265th of the series extant—114 of them have been printed and circulated.

The Chamberlain is the Keeper of the Freemen's Roll. He holds a Court for the presentation of Freedoms, and it is his duty to address and offer the right hand of fellowship to those distinguished persons to whom the Court of Common Council have granted the Honorary Freedom of the City.

The Chamberlain is one of the three Corporation Trustees, and also one of the custodians of the City Seal.

THE TOWN CLERK.

The Town Clerk (originally called the Common Clerk) is an ancient and chartered officer, and forms a component part of the Corporation. The office can be traced in the City Records as far back as the 13th year of the reign of Edward I. A.D. 1284, and by the "constitutions" granted by Edward II. in 1319, it was ordained that "the Common Clerk be chosen by the Commonalty of the City, and be removed according to the will of the same Commonalty."

A few of the duties of the office of the Town Clerk follow :—

To attend the Court of Aldermen, advise the Court on its procedure, conduct its business, and enter on the Minutes and in the Repertories the business transacted by the Court, and issue its orders. To attend the Court of Common Council, advise the Court on its procedure, conduct its business, and

enter on the Minutes and in the Journals the business transacted by the Court. To attend the Common Hall and advise
and minute its proceedings. To attend upon the Lord Mayor
and Aldermen on all public and ceremonial occasions. To
generally advise the Lord Mayor, when so required. To advise
concerning the Laws, Customs, Liberties, and Privileges of
the City. To administer the Oath or Declaration of office to
the Lord Mayor, Aldermen, Sheriffs, and every other person
admitted to any Corporate office. To issue all Precepts to the
several Wards for the annual election of Common Councilmen
and Ward Officers, and to the different Companies of the City
to assemble in Common Hall. He is one of the three Corporation Trustees. To provide a book or schedule and fairly
enter therein an account of all the Charters, Records,
Repertories, Journals, and other Muniments, Books, and Documents, belonging to the City, in his official custody, and to
sign the same and verify the receipt thereof within three
calendar months next after his appointment to the office, and
to keep the same, at all times, in safe custody in the Muniment
Rooms provided by the Corporation for that purpose.

Muniment Rooms.

On entering one of the muniment rooms, one is brought
face to face with some of the more cherished of all the CITY's
ARCHIVES. The well-known *Liber Albus* or White Book
of the City, being a compilation made early in the
15th century by John Carpenter—sometime Town Clerk
of the City, and founder of the City of London School—
of ordinances, customs, and charters that have regulated
the government of the City from time immemorial. Here
also is the scarcely less famous *Liber Custumarum*, or
Book of Customs of the City of an earlier date, being
of the 14th century, whilst in close proximity stands a
MS. of still earlier date—indeed, the earliest of all the volumes
here treasured—viz., the volume known as the *Liber de*

Antiquis Legibus, compiled A.D. 1274. Two other compilations bear the names of two high officers of the Corporation. These are (1) *Liber Horn*, so called from having been compiled by Andrew Horn, who, besides being a citizen and fishmonger, was also an eminent jurist, and at one time Chamberlain of the City; and (2) *Liber Dunthorn*, called after a Town Clerk of the 15th century. The *Liber Horn* bears date A.D. 1311. On the shelves immediately adjoining, lie—row upon row—the Rolls of the Court of Husting from A.D. 1253, and these may be seen occupying the upper shelves round three parts of the room. Under them, and round the greater part of the room, stand the " Journals," or Transactions of the Court of Common Council of the City, and above these the " Repertories," or Minutes of the Court of Aldermen. The increasing size of the Journals as the years roll on, affords striking evidence of the increased work of the Corporation.

THE COMMON SERJEANT.

This Office is one of great antiquity, and the date of its creation is not precisely known, but it is, like the office of Town Clerk, named in the "Constitutions" of 1319. The Common Serjeant attends at the Sessions House, Old Bailey, during the whole of the sittings of the Central Criminal Court, and presides as one of the Judges. In the unavoidable absence of the Recorder, he charges the Grand Jury. He also sits, in the absence of the Recorder, as one of the Judges of the Lord Mayor's Court. He attends the Common Hall, and, in the absence of the Recorder, advises the Livery. He also submits the names of candidates at the elections of Lord Mayor, Sheriffs, Chamberlain, Bridge-Masters, Auditors, and other Officers of the Livery, and reports to the Court of Aldermen, in the name of the Sheriffs (whose adviser he is on the occasion), the results of the different elections. He attends the Lord Mayor upon all public and Ceremonial occasions. He is one of the Law Officers of the Corporation.

Until the passing of the Local Government Act, 1888, the election to this office rested with the Common Council, but by that Act, all future appointments were vested in the Crown, but the privilege of fixing the salary and of defining the duties of the office still remains with the Corporation.

THE COMPTROLLER.

The Comptroller of the Chamber, who is also Vice-Chamberlain, holds an ancient office, which was in existence prior to the reign of Edward I. He is the custodian of the title deeds, leases, plans, &c., of the City's property. He is the Conveyancing Officer of the Corporation. The following is a list of some of the duties performed by him :—

He is required to attend the Court of Aldermen, and the Court of Common Council upon all occasions, and to attend the Lord Mayor at Common Halls, and upon all public and ceremonial occasions. To act as Vice-Chamberlain, whenever the Chamberlain is prevented by illness or other cause, and during a vacancy in the office of Chamberlain. To keep in safe custody the title deeds, leases, plans and other documents of, and relating to, the City and Bridge-House Estates, and the several markets of the Corporation. To complete the general rental of the City and Bridge-House Estates, the accounts of fines and premiums received for leases ; to attend the Auditors of the City and Bridge-House Accounts ; to produce and examine the said rentals, &c., as a check against the Chamberlain. To prepare and examine all leases. To draw and sign all money bonds and securities, and prepare coupons to the same, when ordered. To investigate all titles, prepare all deeds, conveyances, contracts and agreements relating to estates purchased by the Corporation, in whatever capacity. The Comptroller is one of the three Corporation Trustees, a law officer of the Corporation, and one of the three Custodians of the City Seal.

The City Remembrancer.

The duties of the office of Remembrancer are divided into three classes, viz : Ceremonial, Parliamentary, and Legal. The office has been filled continuously from Elizabethan times, and although it was originally, and continued for many years to be of a ceremonial and secretarial character only, it apparently involved constant communication with the Court and Ministers. In the year 1685, an order was made for the Remembrancer to continue to attend Parliament and the offices of the Secretaries of State daily, and acquaint the Lord Mayor with the public affairs and other business transacted there, relating to the City. The ceremonial duties of the office involve all the arrangements necessary to be made upon the presentation of addresses from the Corporation to the Crown, the Members of the Royal Family, or to either House of Parliament, the Corporation being entitled to exceptional privileges on these occasions, for the due maintenance of which the Remembrancer is responsible. On the demise of the Crown, the Remembrancer has to take measures with respect to the Accession and Proclamation of the Successor. He has also to attend the Court of Claims appointed at Coronations, make the claims of the Lord Mayor and citizens, obtain their allowance and receive the orders in relation to the execution of them, and to attend the Lord Mayor to St. James' Palace. On the election of a Lord Mayor, he makes the necessary appointment and arrangements for the presentation of the Lord Mayor Elect to the Lord Chancellor, when the Sovereign's approbation is signified. On occasions of public thanksgiving and funerals, he takes the requisite measures for preserving the privileges and due precedence of the Corporation in Procession and Cathedral. He invites the Members of the Royal Family and the great Officers of State to the Guildhall Banquet on the 9th November, and has to arrange the reception of the company in the Library and their seating in the Hall, and to perform similar duties on the occasions of other Entertainments in Guildhall. On the occasion of the Sovereign entering the City, he attends at the offices of the Lord Chamberlain and the Master of the Horse, to make the necessary arrangements connected with the ancient ceremony of surrendering the Sword.

The Parliamentary duties of the Remembrancer involve a daily attendance at the Houses of Parliament, during the Session, and require a constant watching of all measures introduced, or proposed to be introduced, in order that the Corporation may be informed of all matters likely to affect its interests, which he duly reports. For this purpose, the officials of both Houses of Parliament give him facilities of admission and attendance, and he enjoys the privilege of a seat under the gallery.

The Remembrancer is one of the Law Officers of the Corporation, and it is his duty, with his colleagues, to advise the Corporation, or any of its Committees, on such points of law as they may at any time desire to submit.

THE CITY SOLICITOR.

Although this office is not of so ancient an origin as some of those already dealt with, it nevertheless appears from the City's Records that the first appointment thereto was made by the Court of Aldermen so long ago as the year 1545. Since the year 1755 to the present time, the City Solicitor has been appointed by the Court of Common Council, and is now subject to annual election. The duties pertaining to the office consisted from the earliest times in conducting all legal proceedings on the part of the Corporation.

The following are a few of the duties of the office :— To act as the Lord Mayor's Assessor at Wardmotes. To conduct all proceedings whatever, at law and in equity, to which the Corporation is a party, and such other general business as he may be ordered to do by the Court of Aldermen, the Court of Common Council, or by the Committees appointed by those Courts, and to attend, when necessary, all meetings of such Courts or Committees. To prepare all Acts of Common Council, Bye-laws and Regulations, and prosecute parties for disobeying the same. To prosecute persons presented by the Inquests of the several Wards of the City for various offences and nuisances. To defend the Magistrates and Officers of the City in proceedings instituted against them for acts done in the execution of their respective offices and the discharge of their several duties, and to prosecute persons for assaults on Police and other Constables of the City and other Civil Officers, in the execution of their duty. To prosecute and bring to justice all such persons as the Court of Aldermen, the Lord Mayor, or the Sitting Magistrates, for the time being, may think proper to order to be prosecuted, where no public fund is provided for the purpose, and in cases where, from the parties being unable of themselves to prosecute, the delinquents would otherwise escape justice.

To attend before the Queen's Remembrancer to render ancient service, on behalf of the Corporation, in connection with certain property held of the Crown. He also acts as Legal Adviser to the Commissioner of the City Police, to the Visiting Committee of the City of London Lunatic Asylum; and is one of the Law Officers of the Corporation. The duties of this Officer have recently been very considerably augmented, consequent upon the absorption of the Commissioners of Sewers.

The Secondary.

The office of Secondary is another ancient Civic Office, the holder of it performing all the duties which ordinarily attach to an Under-Sheriff; the term "Secondary" being synonymous with that of Under-Sheriff.

The office of Secondary is held direct from the Corporation, which is liable to the Crown for any misconduct on the part of the Sheriffs, Secondary, and Sheriff's Officers. The Sheriffs, personally, derive no pecuniary benefit from their office, and they and the Corporation are indemnified against loss by the Secondary, who gives a Bond to the Corporation, himself in an unlimited amount and with two Sureties jointly and severally bound in the sum of £2,500, to efficiently discharge all the duties devolving upon him as the representative of the Sheriffs ; his official place of business being called ' the Office of the Sheriffs of London.'

THE CITY SURVEYOR.

This officer was formerly designated Clerk of the City's Works, and was altered in 1848 to Architect and Surveyor, but at the time of the last appointment in 1891 the designation was altered to that of City Surveyor. His duties include attendance on the Courts of Aldermen, Courts of Common Council and Committees, whenever required ; making surveys and valuations of all Corporation Estates whether Trust Property or otherwise, advising as to the letting of all property, preparing plans, surveying all property, directing all works of repair to public buildings and property of the Corporation, preparing designs for new buildings, performing such work and duties as may arise out of Acts of Parliament in which the Corporation may have an interest, and generally performing the usual duties of an Architect and Surveyor.

The Court of Aldermen.

IN early times the Aldermen seem to have had a kind of proprietary right over their Wards, arising no doubt from the fact that many of them were territorial magnates, this would probably account for the singularly irregular boundaries of many of the City Wards. In the possession of the Dean and Chapter of St. Paul's, there is a document of the early part of the twelfth century in which the names, description and Wards of many of the Aldermen are given; for instance, we find the Ward of Godwin, son of Esgar; the Ward of Edward Parole; the Ward of Brichmar the Moneyer; the Ward of Osbert Dringepinne and the Ward of Brocesgange; later on (1276) we find the Tower Ward called the Ward of William de Hadestock; Vintry Ward the Ward of Henry de Coventre; and Farringdon Ward, previously known as the Ward of Ludgate and Newgate, and also as the Ward of Anketin de Auvergne. It obtains its present name from William de Farringdon or Farndon, its Alderman, whose son-in-law Nicholas devised the Aldermanry to John de Pulteneye.

The first mention of a "Court of Aldermen" is found in an ancient chronicle where the writer, himself an Alderman, says:

"In the year 1200 were chosen five and twenty of the more discreet men of the City, and sworn to take counsel on behalf of the City, together with the Mayor."

The City (described by Lord Coke as *Epitome totius regni*) appears to have been governed by the Court of Aldermen before the Common Council was in existence.

In 1319, the King declared that all the Aldermen should be removed each year and not be re-elected. This gave rise to some trouble. From 1377 to 1393, however, each Ward annually elected its own Alderman, after which, the Aldermen for the time being retained their office for life, unless removed therefrom for some reasonable and justifiable cause ; and this rule continues to the present day. The following is the old oath administered to an Alderman on taking office :—

"THE OTHE OF THE ALDERMEN."

" Ye shall sweare that ye shall well and lawfully serve our Soveraigne Lady the Queen, in the Citty of London, in the office of Alderman, in the Ward of ———, whereof ye be chosen Alderman, and every other Ward whereof ye shalbe chosen Alderman hereafter. And lawfully ye shall entreate the people of the same Ward of such things as to them perteyneth to doe, for keping of the Citty, and for maynteyning of the peace in the same. And the Lawes and Franchises of this Citty ye shall keepe and mayntayne, within the Citty and without ; after your witt and power. And attendant ye shalbe to mayntayne the right of Orphans, after the Lawes and Usages of the same Citty. And ready ye shalbe to com at the sommons and warnings of the Maior and Mynisters of this Citty for the tyme being, to speede th' Assises, Plees, and Judgements of the Hustings, and other needs of this Citty, yf ye be not lett by the needs of the Queen, or by some other reasonable cause, and good and lawful counsell ye shall give for such things as towch the comon proffitt of the Citty. And ye shall sell no manner victual by retayle, as breade, ale, wyne, flesh ne fysh, by your apprentices, allowes, servaunts, ne by any other way. Ne proffit shall ye none take of any such manner victuall so sould during your office. The secrets of this Court ye shall keepe, and not disclose any thing here spoken, for the comon wealth of this Citty, or that might hurt any person or brother of this said Courte, unlesse it be spoken to your brother, or to any other which in your conscience and discretion ye shall thinck to be for the comon wealth of this Citty. And well and lawfully ye shall behave you in the sayd office, and in all other things towching the said Citty.

As God you helpe."

The inhabitants on the Electoral Roll (practically the Parliamentary Voting List) of each of the twenty-five Wards have the right to elect a Freeman to be their Alderman. The election is conducted (by ballot) precisely as at an election for a member of Parliament. Before an Alderman can take his seat as such he must be approved and admitted by the Court of Aldermen. Should the electors of any Ward return a person who has been adjudged and determined by the Court of Aldermen to be unfit to support the dignity and discharge the duties of the office of Alderman, the Court may, after rejection three times in succession, themselves nominate, elect, and admit a fit and proper person, being a Freeman of the City, to fill the office. Every Alderman of the City of London is, in virtue of his office, a Justice of the Peace for the County of that City, and as such he possesses very extensive powers. Every Alderman may, within his Ward, execute such duties as are allowed to be done and executed by one or two Justices of the Peace of any County. He can also, when sitting at either of the City Justice Rooms do alone, any act, which by any Statute (*past or future*) is directed to be done by more than one Justice, and shall be deemed to be a Court of Summary Jurisdiction consisting of two or more Justices. All the Aldermen are Justices of Oyer and Terminer, and, as such, are named in the Commission for holding the Old Bailey Sessions. They also discharge important duties under the City Police Act, 1839, and the various Licensing Acts.

The Court of Aldermen appoint a number of their body as Visiting Justices of H.M. Prisons of Newgate and Holloway. The Aldermen are, severally, Governors of the Royal Hospitals, viz., St. Bartholomew's, Christ's, Bridewell and Bethlem, and St. Thomas's, and Members of the Police Committee. Each Alderman has the government of his Ward and the appointment of a Deputy from among its Common Councilmen. A person who refuses to serve as Alderman on being elected, is liable to a fine of £500, unless he is in a position to satisfy the Court of Aldermen that at the time of his election he was not worth £30,000.

An Alderman does not wear a Chain of Office until he becomes Sheriff, when he wears one during his term of Shrievalty. After the expiration of that year, he does not wear it again until he has passed the Mayoral Chair, and it is then usual to add the Sword and Mace to the Badge. An Alderman is addressed as Worshipful until he has passed the Mayoral Chair, and afterwards as Right Worshipful.

The duties devolving on a City Alderman, are many and of a most responsible nature—the few already mentioned will give some idea of their general importance.

The Court of Common Council.

THE earliest known list of members of this Council is found in the City Archives *circa* 1285, "the names of the good men of all the Wards sworn to consult with the Aldermen on the affairs of the City of London." This list contains 40 names, another list of 133 names is found in 1347, and in this list the Wards are duly represented, in proportion to their size, by six, five, or fewer representatives. In 1341, King Edward III. granted the City a Charter, empowering the citizens, in their Corporate capacity, to amend customs which, in course of time, should have been found hard or defective. The Guilds, taking advantage of this provision, claimed a more direct participation in the government of the City than they had hitherto enjoyed, with the result that, in 1376 they were able to wrest the election of the members of the Common Council and of the Lord Mayor and Sheriffs from the Wards, and vest it instead in the Guilds.

In less than ten years, however (in 1384), the election had reverted to the inhabitants of the Wards, being Freemen, each Ward electing representatives as before in proportion to its size, and this system has continued down to the present day (except as to the necessity of the Elector being a Freeman). Under the provisions of this Charter (1341) the Court of Common Council has, from time to time, fixed the number of annually elected representatives (at present, 206), has settled the qualifications required both for electors and elected, and has from time to time reformed the machinery of the City's Municipal

Government without objection or interference from authorities outside. Ever since its first institution, it has been and still is, a body exercising legislative as well as executive functions—as an instance—in 1840—when the number of the Common Council was reduced from 240 to 206—and many more instances might be cited.

This Court has also the exclusive power of conferring the honorary freedom of the City, and of voting Corporate addresses to Royal and other distinguished personages. All documents requiring the Common Seal of the Corporation, and also leases granted by the Royal Hospitals (of which the Chamberlain holds the Corporate Seal), must be sealed in open Court, at a meeting of the Common Council. The Court is widely known for its munificent support of public charities, and liberal contributions to the relief of distress in all parts of the world. The majority of the City offices are in the gift of the Common Council, or its various Committees.

Every person eligible as a representative on the Common Council must (first) be a Freeman of the City, and householder in the Ward he seeks to represent, in other words, a person who being free of the City is rated for a house, paying scot and bearing lot. This is the ancient custumal qualification. Or (secondly) he must be a Freeman of the City and must occupy premises to the value of £10 per annum in the Ward he desires to represent, and must be on the annual Register of Parliamentary voters for the City of London, in respect to such premises; this is the statutory qualification. The qualifications of the electors are the same as those required in the candidates, except that the elector need not be a Freeman of the City. The City of London is divided into twenty-five Wards of unequal size, Bassishaw, the smallest, has four representatives, and the largest, Farringdon Without, sixteen, and in addition there is one Ward called " Bridge Without," which has an Alderman, who is elected by the Court of Aldermen from amongst those Aldermen who have served the office of Lord Mayor. It has no other representative. Every Common Councilman ceases to hold office at midnight, on the 20th December, and next day—St. Thomas's Day—the annual elections to fill their places are held at the various 'Wardmotes' presided over by the Alderman of the Ward, or in his unavoidable absence by the Lord Mayor. The Court of Common Council—the full style of which is "the Lord Mayor, Aldermen and Commons of the City of London in Common Council assembled"—consists of the Lord Mayor, 25 other Aldermen, and 206 Commoners, making a total of 232. Party politics have no part in the Municipal Elections of the City ; how to promote the best interests of the Ward and the City, is the paramount consideration in the mind of both the electors and the elected, character and business experience being the only qualities taken into account.

The following was recently written by a public City man respecting the personnel of the Common Council :—

"Any man who will visit the Council Chamber when "the discussions are going on, or who will read them in the "public press, will be fully convinced that a patriotic, generous, "unselfish spirit pervades the debates. There is a marked "absence of personalities and bitterness even during the "warmest contests, and the citizens of London have good "reason to be proud of the men that they send to represent "them."

The following extracts from the Report of the Municipal Corporations Commissioners, 1837, clearly explain why other Corporations were reformed, and the Corporation of London left to continue unaltered its beneficent career :—

"We therefore feel it to be our duty to represent to your Majesty that the existing Municipal Corporations of England and Wales neither possess nor deserve the confidence or respect of your Majesty's subjects, and that a thorough reform must be effected before they can become, what we humbly submit to your Majesty they ought to be, useful and efficient instruments of local government."

"The history of the Common Council of London is that of a body which has watched vigilantly over the interests of its constituents, and for a long series of years has studied to improve the Corporate Institutions with great earnestness, unremitting caution, and scrupulous justice."

the result of the Report being that the Corporation was left the only unreformed Corporation in the Kingdom. Whenever reform has been found necessary, the Common Council itself has always effected such reform. The entire absence of political controversy, in its debates and elections, has undoubtedly tended to make the Corporation an Institution to which both parties of the State can have recourse, with the certainty that no question of international importance is likely to be disregarded or receive inadequate or partial consideration at its hands.

Always anxious to maintain its ancient traditions and privileges unsullied and uncurtailed, its Members perform, daily, important Municipal functions, with humble reliance upon the City's time-honoured Motto, *Domine dirige nos.*

The Corporation's connection with Other Public Bodies.

IT is not generally known that, in addition to the work of the Corporation of London in managing its own affairs, it is associated with many other bodies in carrying out public work. Among these may be mentioned :—

THE ROYAL HOSPITALS,

which were founded by Charter of Edward VI., and endowed by the Corporation, and of which the Right Hon. the Lord Mayor is the head (with the exception of Christ's).

These Hospitals are :—St. Bartholomew's, Christ's, Bridewell and Bethlehem, and St. Thomas's. All the Aldermen and twelve Commoners are Governors of each of these Hospitals.

THE THAMES CONSERVANCY BOARD,

to which the Corporation send two Aldermen and four Commoners as representatives.

THE RIVER LEA CONSERVANCY,

to which one representative is sent.

THE CITY AND GUILDS INSTITUTE.

The Lord Mayor, the Recorder, six Aldermen, and twelve Commoners are members of the Board of Governors.

THE CITY OF LONDON PAROCHIAL CHARITIES.

Four members are sent by the Corporation to serve on the Governing Body.

The Mitchell City of London Charity.

This is a Charity managed by fifteen trustees, of whom four represent the Corporation. It consists of a sum of £90,000, bequeathed in 1876 by Mr. T. A. Mitchell, M.P.

Under a scheme of the Court of Chancery, 1883, one-third of the income is devoted to the relief of the poor of the City of London, grants to dispensaries, pensions, &c. The remaining two-thirds are devoted to educational purposes for the benefit of persons resident in, or engaged, or employed, in the City of London, and their children.

The London Chamber of Arbitration.

The object of this Chamber is " the speedy and inexpensive settlement of disputes arising in the course of business without having recourse to litigation."

It is under the control of a Joint Committee of Management of twelve members, viz., six appointed by the Corporation and six by the London Chamber of Commerce. The fees are very low, and the rules admit of a very speedy and economical settlement of disputes. The rules can be obtained at the Guildhall.

The Lieutenancy of London.

The Lieutenancy of the City of London is a Commission named by the Crown and issued under the Privy Seal, under an Act passed in 1673.

The Commission consists of the Lord Mayor, the Aldermen, the Recorder, the Chamberlain, the Town Clerk, the Common Sergeant, and the Aldermen's Deputies. The Lord Mayor has also the privilege of recommending to Her Majesty, for approval by the Secretary of State for War, eminent merchants and citizens for inclusion in the Commission.

The powers of the Lieutenancy, as regards the Militia and the Rifle Volunteer Corps of the City of London, are precisely similar to those of Lords Lieutenants of counties. Its expenses are met by means of a trophy tax, levied on the Wards.

The Work of the Common Council.

HAVING now described the Guildhall, the Ceremonies, Officials, Insignia, and given a history of the Courts of Aldermen and Common Council, it now remains, as indicated in the preface of this Guide, to give an account of the work carried on in Guildhall in the government of the "one square mile."

The work of the Corporation is chiefly carried on by means of a number of Committees, which are entrusted with certain powers, but which are required to report to the Court of Common Council on all important matters, receiving its sanction before putting the same into execution. Among other matters, all lettings of property must be submitted to the Court for approval. The composition and formation of these Committees is as follows :—

Every Committee of the Common Council (with the exception of two or three which will be specially mentioned) consists of six Aldermen and 29 Commoners ; the first named are nominated by the Court of Aldermen, and the Commoners by the members for the 25 Wards (or sides of Wards), each nominating one of their number to the Court of Common Council, which usually confirms such nominations. Subject to annual re-election on St. Thomas' Day, each member serves for four years, and cannot continue longer to be a member of the same Committee unless with the consent of all his colleagues in his Ward, and also with the approbation of the Court of Common Council. This rule acts most beneficially, ensuring as it does,

that, by passing from one committee to another, members
obtain a general knowledge of all branches of Corporation work.
A chairman is elected at the first meeting of the Committee
in each year and acts for the year, and only in most exceptional
cases is the term extended, but he remains (as late Chairman)
a member of the Committee for another year.

Photo by the L. S. & P. Co., Ld.

A COMMITTEE ROOM.

The work of the Committees may be conveniently divided
under five heads : (1) Estates and Management ; (2) Educational ; (3) Open Spaces ; (4) Administration ; (5) Public
Health. The Committees in charge of each section under
these heads are as follows :—

Under the first head—The City Lands, Bridge House
Estates, the Irish Society, Coal and Corn and Finance, Law
and City Courts, Officers and Clerks, General Purposes, and
the Special.

Under the second head—The Gresham, Library and Art Gallery, City of London Schools, Music, and Orphan School.

Under the third head—Epping Forest, West Ham Park, and Coal and Corn and Finance.

Under the fourth head—Markets, Police, County Purposes, Port of London Sanitary ; and under the fifth head—Improvements and Finance, Streets, Sanitary and Accounts.

ESTATES AND MANAGEMENT.

THE CITY LANDS COMMITTEE.

This Committee is the premier one of the Corporation, not only by reason of its antiquity, but by the importance of its work. The members comprising it have usually served upon most of the other committees. The Chairman is designated " Chief Commoner " of the Court of Common Council during his year of office, and as such is the spokesman of the Court on all official occasions. Upon this Committee devolves the management of the Lands and Buildings belonging to the Corporation, with the exception of the few which fall within the special province of other Committees.

The Revenue derived from the Corporate Estates forms, mainly, the Fund which is known as the City's Cash, out of which all the ordinary expenses of Civic Government are paid. Among these expenses may be mentioned those connected with the Mayoralty, the Official Staff, the Central Criminal Court, the Magistracy, the Coroner, the Mayor's Court, the Guildhall and offices and buildings connected therewith, and also a contribution of one fourth part of the expenses of the City Police force, this amounting on an average to about £33,000 per annum. The net average revenue for the last three years of the City's Estate is about £138,000 per annum, and the average annual rental of the property for the same period under the control of the Committee amounts, in the gross, to about £181,000.

The number of houses belonging to the Corporation under the control of this Committee (including weekly lettings), is 2,514. The number of leases is about 1,256.

As stated in an old Minute Book of the reign of Charles II., it has been the custom, from time immemorial, on the expiration of leases, to give the occupying tenants the first refusal of renewals, at rents determined by the Committee.

This Committee, besides the letting, control, and management of the Corporation Estates (as before mentioned), has the charge of the Guildhall, the Monument (which is annually visited by about 50,000 persons); and all the other monuments in the public streets belonging to the Corporation; the management of the Bunhill Fields Burial Ground, the City Greenyard (used for stabling horses or other animals belonging to individuals in charge of the police), and the Artizans' Dwellings erected by the Corporation. The Sessions House, Old Bailey, in which is carried on the work of the Central Criminal Court (the most important criminal court in the Kingdom), is also under its control and management. Plans for the erection of a new Sessions House are in course of preparation, under the superintendence of this Committee.

THE BRIDGE-HOUSE ESTATES COMMITTEE.

This Committee has the control of what are known as the Bridge House Estates, out of which are maintained London, Blackfriars, Southwark, and the Tower Bridges.

The real estate of the Bridge-House Trust consists of messuages, lands, and hereditaments situate in the City of London, the Borough of Southwark, and the counties of Surrey, Kent, and Essex, a considerable part of which is let on lease. The number of houses, &c., under the management of the Committee is about 2,414, of which 497 are shops and offices, 29 wharves, &c., 23 warehouses, 80 stables, and 1,785 houses.

The title of the Corporation of London to the Bridge-House Estates is very ancient ; and the property was generally granted and devised by the Kings of England and "charitable and well-disposed persons," and is held by the Mayor and Commonalty and citizens of the City of London upon Trust, primarily for the maintenance and support of London Bridge ; the words used in the conveyances and grants being generally " to the use of London Bridge," "for the works of London Bridge," or "for the sustentation of London Bridge." The Comptroller, the Conveyancing Officer of the Corporation, has in his custody grants and conveyances as early as 1282 and 1288, containing the above words, and also Leases granted by the Corporation, prior to those dates. In 1274(Edward I.), a Commission was issued to enquire into the revenues, &c., of the Bridge-House Estates, and the Inquisition under that Commission found that the custody of the revenues of the Bridge-House Estates had always belonged to the City and citizens of London. The annual rental of the Bridge-House Estates amounted at Christmas, 1898, to nearly £99,000, and the charges thereon (exclusive of the repayment of Loans), amount to about £53,000 per annum. The average annual charge for the maintenance and support of London Bridge, Southwark Bridge, Blackfriars Bridge, and the Tower Bridge (including the expenses attendant upon paving, watching, lighting, cleansing, and watering the same) is £25,000. The expenses connected with the building and maintenance of these bridges have been about two-and-a-half millions sterling. A short account of these four bridges may be interesting :—

LONDON BRIDGE.

A low wooden bridge was in existence across the Thames at St. Botolph's Wharf so long ago as the year 944, and in 1176 the foundation of the first stone bridge was laid, the building of which occupied some 33 years, the opening taking place in 1209. This bridge stood the wear and tear of nearly seven centuries.

In 1755, an Act of Parliament was passed for improving, widening and enlarging the bridge, the new works necessitating the pulling down of the old houses which, for many years, had stood upon it. In 1767, the removal of the tolls, formerly levied on the bridge, cost the Corporation £30,000. In 1823, it at last became necessary to entirely rebuild the Bridge, and, to enable this to be done, a further Act was obtained. In 1825, the construction of the present bridge was commenced. It was opened by King William IV., on the 1st August 1831, and cost, with its immediate approaches, £715,246.

BLACKFRIARS BRIDGE.

This bridge was originally constructed by the Corporation under the powers of an Act passed in 1755, at a cost of some £230,000, a portion of which was authorised to be raised upon the tolls the Corporation was empowered to levy, and the balance upon the security of the Bridge-House Estates. In repairing this bridge, an expenditure of £105,158 became necessary, which was provided by the Bridge-House Estates. The bridge remained in use for nearly a century ; but, in 1863, having become unsafe, and it being anticipated that it would be still further endangered by the Embankment on the northern side of the river, then about to be constructed, Parliament sanctioned the rebuilding of the bridge, and the Blackfriars Bridge Act, 1863, was passed for that purpose. The Corporation was authorised to raise, on the credit of the Bridge-House Estates, the sum of £300,000. The work was commenced in June, 1864, and the first stone laid 20th July, 1865. It was completed and opened for traffic by Her Majesty the Queen, on the 7th November, 1869, the total cost amounting to £401,131.

SOUTHWARK BRIDGE.

This bridge was erected by a company incorporated under the name of the " Southwark Bridge Company " in the year

1811. In 1865, an Act of Parliament was passed authorising the sale or transfer of Southwark Bridge to the Corporation, on such terms as might be arranged between the Company and the Corporation. An arrangement was entered into between the Company and the Corporation, by which the bridge was acquired by the latter and opened "free of toll" on the 8th November, 1864. In 1867, the Corporation was empowered by Statute to raise the necessary purchase-money on the security of the Bridge-House Estates, and the purchase was completed in the year 1868 for the sum of £218,868, and by the same Act the Bridge-House Estates were charged with the maintenance and support of this bridge.

THE TOWER BRIDGE.

The enormously increased vehicular traffic across London and Southwark Bridges (in 1884, nearly 28,000 vehicles passed over the former in one day) and the serious lack of bridge accommodation below London Bridge became in recent years the subject-matter of almost daily complaint ; at the same time, there was a growing dislike on the part of those responsible for the provision of additional means of access between the north and south sides of the Thames, outside the City boundaries, to incur the necessary expenditure, which would, of course, seriously add to the already sufficiently large Metropolitan rates. In 1884, the Corporation, after exhaustive enquiry, acceded to the public demand, and caused the necessary Parliamentary Notices to be given of the promotion of a Bill in the then ensuing Session of Parliament, empowering the Corporation to erect a bridge on a site (Irongate Stairs) immediately adjacent to the southern boundary of the Tower on the north side or the Thames, and to Hartley's Wharf, Horselydown, on the south side of the Thames. The Bridge was commenced building in 1886, from the designs of Sir Horace Jones, the City Architect (who died shortly afterwards) ; Mr. John Wolfe Barry, C.E., being the engineer responsible for the

NORTHERN APPROACH TO THE TOWER BRIDGE.　　EARLY MORNING.

construction. On the 30th June, 1894, H.R.H. The Prince
of Wales (who had laid the foundation stone), accompanied
by the Princess of Wales, opened the Bridge on behalf
of Her Majesty the Queen. The conclusions formed as

to the necessity for further provisions for cross-river traffic below London Bridge were amply justified from the first day of the opening of the Bridge. From the 9th July to the 9th September, 1894, a total of 3,441,572 foot passengers and 358,404 vehicles passed over the bridge—giving a daily average of 54,628 foot passengers and 5,688 vehicles. The vehicular traffic has since largely increased, as on one day, in 1895, 8,751, and in 1897, 9,901 vehicles passed over the bridge. The marked relief afforded to the traffic of London Bridge is a matter of common observation: The total cost, with the approaches, amounted to £1,200,000. The annual cost of maintenance is £15,000.

It will be noted that these four bridges have been built or purchased and are maintained out of the "Bridge House Estate Trust" fund, administered by the Corporation, and that the ratepayers have never been called upon for the smallest contribution.

In connection with the care of the bridges are two Bridge Masters, elected annually in Common Hall on Midsummer Day, by the Mayor, Aldermen and Liverymen of the several City Livery Companies, their principal duty is to daily inspect and report monthly to the Bridge-House Estates Committee on the condition of London, Southwark and Blackfriars Bridges. The office is one of the most ancient in the Corporation.

THE IRISH SOCIETY.

Although the business of the "Irish Society" is not managed by the Common Council, it is thought that, as all the Members are appointed by that body, an account of the Society and its work may appropriately be mentioned.

The "Irish Society" consists of a Governor (who must be an Alderman) Deputy-Governor, and twenty-four Assistants, six Assistants, including the Governor, being Aldermen of the City (the Recorder being also an Assistant), and the Deputy-

Governor and the remainder of the Assistants being Common Councilmen. In February, in each year 12 new Members are elected by the Common Council to take the place of the same number retiring after two years' service.

The connection of the Corporation with the Estates in the Province of Ulster over which the Irish Society now exercises control, began in the year 1609, in the reign of James I. Owing to divisions between two great families (the O'Neils and O'Dohertys) who, in the reign of Queen Elizabeth, divided between them the whole of the Province of Ulster, with the exception of the Counties Down and Antrim, and who were in constant rebellion against the English Crown, the whole of their estates were forfeited to the Crown.

Two Commissioners were appointed, in 1602 and 1609, to enquire into the title of the Crown to the escheated lands, and Inquisitions were duly held to ascertain and define those that were forfeited, together with the rights, privileges, and fisheries appertaining thereto, and a project was set on foot for establishing a Protestant Colony on the same, which received the King's approval. Certain conditions were thereupon laid down for observance by the Privy Council, and the English and Scotch people were invited to undertake the necessary work. The public, however, not responding to this invitation, King James directed the Earl of Salisbury, Lord High Treasurer, who had first conceived the project of Protestant colonization, to write to the then City Remembrancer (Sir Clement Edmonds), asking for a conference on the subject, and the Lord Mayor appointed a deputation to consider the matter. After the lapse of a few days, the Lords of the Privy Council and the Corporation of London came to an understanding, and the Corporation expressed its willingness to undertake the plantation, and on the 1st August, 1609, the Court of Common Council appointed four representatives to proceed to Ireland to view the site of the proposed Colony, and report their proceedings and opinions thereon.

After the return of the Deputation, the Court of Common Council appointed a Committee to confer with the Privy Council, and after considerable negotiation, Articles of Agreement were (on the 28th January, 1610) entered into between the Privy Council and the Corporation. These Articles included the raising by the City of £20,000, the rebuilding of Derry ; the rebuilding of Coleraine ; the buying up of all interests, &c. ; and the Corporation were to be put in possession of the Estates; to have the patronage of all Churches in Derry and Coleraine ; the Customs for ninety-nine years ; the Office of Admiralty ; Salmon and Eel fishings of the River Bann and Lough Foyle, and other rights of fishing were to be granted in perpetuity to the City.

Letters Patent were subsequently granted, embodying the constitution of the Society as above set out, and the Society was put in possession of the Estates. The Corporation raised the £20,000 named in the Articles of Agreement by an assessment on the City Companies (which subsequently had portions of the Estate granted to them), but this amount being found insufficient, further assessments were made, and the amount raised eventually exceeded £60,000, a very large sum of money in those days. About the year 1615, these Estates (except the City of Londonderry, the Town of Coleraine, and their contiguous lands, and the woods, forests and fisheries, which were retained by the Society), were conveyed to the respective chief Companies, according to allotment based upon the contributions of the various Companies, and conveyances were executed by the Society, in 1617, to the chief Companies, of the lands so allotted.

The City of Londonderry and Town of Coleraine, with the lands attached thereto, and the woods, forests, and fisheries, were retained by the Society.

The Irish Society, in addition to re-building Derry, fortified it, and at the first Siege of Derry (1643) sent four ships to its relief, with provisions, clothing, accoutrements, and ammunition. Each of the twelve chief City Companies also sent two pieces of ordnance.

The Society's property consists of the City of Derry, with 4,000 acres, the Town of Coleraine, with 3,000 acres, the Lands of Culmore, containing about 470 acres, and the Rivers Foyle and Bann.

The revenue derived therefrom averages some £18,000 per annum, the whole of which, after providing for cost of management, is expended on the property.

With the Society's help, great public improvements have, from time to time, been carried out ; among the more recent may be mentioned, the freeing from toll the Bridge over the Foyle at Derry, towards which the Society contributed £40,000 ; the removal of the bar of sand at the mouth of the River Bann, at a cost to the Society of £40,000 ; the erection of the Society's National Schools at Coleraine, providing for the free education of between 600 and 700 children, which Institution ranks amongst the first in the North of Ireland. Handsome endowments have been granted to Foyle College and St. Columb's College at Derry, and the Academical Institution at Coleraine, whilst the various Churches, Schools and Charities connected with the Districts constantly receive valuable help from the Society's funds.

The Society has also, lately, presented a new Guildhall to the Londonderry Corporation, to whom grants amounting to over £1,200 are made annually.

THE COAL AND CORN AND FINANCE COMMITTEE.

This Committee, as its name imports, is the Finance Committee of the Corporation, and its members have also the

management of several open spaces, described on page 184. Notwithstanding its designation, the Coal and Corn and Finance
Committee has now little to do with either coal or corn, owing
to the abolition of the Coal Duties. The provisions of the
Metage on Grain Act (under which the funds for open spaces
are raised) are carried out by this Committee. The Committee
has the control of the Coal Exchange, which is a public
market, and of the fruit metage under the rights possessed
by the Corporation in virtue of its charters. All
questions of finance and of applications for grants for
the preservation of open spaces are referred to this Committee,
including the raising of money and the paying off of Bonds ;
and by the 51st Standing Order of the Court of Common
Council no proposal in any way affecting the City Estates
(other than the granting or renewal of leases) can be
entertained until it has been submitted to the Committee ; and
no street improvements, public works, or entertainment can be
undertaken beyond the cost of one hundred guineas, unless
the Committee has first reported thereon. All petitions for
grants of money are referred to this Committee, and the
amount to be annually devoted to charitable objects, after a
report from it, is fixed by the Court of Common Council.

The Law and City Courts Committee.

To this Committee are referred the management and supervision of two of the City Law Courts, namely, the Mayor's
Court and the City of London Court, the appointment of
Clerks, &c. Under its supervision, the City of London
Court (owing to the requirements of its increased and increasing
business) has been rebuilt, and still more recently, further
enlarged. To this Committee is also referred the consideration
of all Bills introduced into Parliament affecting the two Courts
above-mentioned, or their procedure or jurisdiction. The
Committee also examines the Secondary's accounts, and

Sheriffs' charges in respect of the preparation of Lists of Voters for Parliamentary and Common Hall Elections in the City.

THE OFFICERS AND CLERKS COMMITTEE.

This Committee has, speaking generally, the supervision of the Corporation Staff, save where the members of the same are specially allocated otherwise ; it has the appointment, or confirmation, of many of the Clerks, Messengers, &c., either with or without the nomination or appointment of the heads of the various departments. It deals, also, with the question of salaries, promotions, superannuations, &c., and generally supervises matters connected therewith.

THE GENERAL PURPOSES COMMITTEE.

This Committee has referred to it all matters relating to the furniture and equipment of the establishment of the Lord Mayor's official residence (the Mansion House), its cleansing, repairing, lighting, &c. Questions affecting the Union of City Benefices in which the Corporation is concerned, are also referred to this Committee, which likewise deals with the enforcement of the Act of Common Council of 1838 with reference to the licensing of carts ; the printing and stationery contracts of all branches of the Corporation, the providing "suitable gold boxes" or "swords of honour" on the conferring of Honorary Freedoms, the compilation and revision of Standing Orders, when references are made by the Court of Common Council for that purpose, and all other matters and things not specifically referred to any other committee.

THE SPECIAL COMMITTEE.

This Committee was established to consider and take action on any Bill or Motion in Parliament or other measure or matter which might be introduced or arise affecting the City, and in this connection it has had various references made to it of very great importance affecting the interests of the citizens.

EDUCATIONAL.

THE COMMITTEE ON GRESHAM AFFAIRS.

This Committee is a joint committee of 24 members, appointed in equal proportions by the Corporation and the Mercers' Company. Sir Thomas Gresham, by his will dated the 5th July, 1575, devised one moiety of the Royal Exchange to the Mayor and Commonalty and citizens of London, and the other moiety to the Wardens and Commonalty of the Mystery of Mercers upon condition (*inter alia*) that the City of London should distribute annually to four persons to lecture on Divinity, Astronomy, Music, and Geometry, £200, being £50 to each ; and that the Company of Mercers should distribute annually to three persons to lecture on Law, Physic, and Rhetoric, £150, being £50 to each. In 1666, the Royal Exchange was destroyed by fire, and it was rebuilt by the Corporation and the Mercers' Company at a cost of £80,000. It was again destroyed by fire in the year 1838, and the joint committee borrowed £190,000 for the rebuilding—a considerable portion of the City's moiety is still outstanding. In 1844, the new Royal Exchange was opened by Her Majesty, the Queen. A further sum of £20,000 was expended in 1884, in roofing in the Quadrangle. In 1844 Gresham College was built at the corner of Gresham and Basinghall Streets at a cost of £14,000. The College contains a large Lecture Hall, capable of holding some 600 persons. Three courses of lectures are delivered by Professors in the autumn, summer, and spring of each year, on the subjects mentioned in Sir Thomas Gresham's will. These lectures are all free to the public, are advertised in the public press and are well attended. Each Lecturer now receives £100 per annum.

The annual income of the estate is about £19,000, chiefly derived from the rents of shops and offices in the Royal Exchange, one moiety belonging to the Mercers' Company and the other to the Corporation. After paying the expenses in

M

connection with the Royal Exchange, and Gresham College, the balance of the City's moiety is allocated to the support of the eight Gresham Almshouses at Brixton, and the eight Almsfolk, and the reduction of the debt contracted by the Corporation for the re-building of the Exchange in 1844. In the Ambulatory of the Exchange is a series of panels which, by the munificence of public bodies and of individuals, are being filled in with pictures typifying Liberty, Commerce, and Education. Seven panels are now completed, and several others are in progress.

The Library Committee.

The Guildhall Library, Reading Room, Museum, and Fine Art Gallery are under the management and control of this Committee, and to it are referred all questions relating to Literature and Art, the purchase of books, medals, antiquities, &c., the control and publication of the City records, the striking of medals, and the general supervision of all matters of a cognate character. An account of the Library is given on previous pages. The annual amount spent in this work, including the expenses of the Art Gallery, is about £7,500.

The City of London Schools Committee.

This Committee has the entire management and control of both the Boys' and the Girls' Schools, and makes an annual report to the Court of Common Council thereon. The Secretaries of the School, the Assistant Masters, and the occasional Masters are appointed by the Committee. The Head Master and Second Master, and the Head Mistress are in the appointment of the Court of Common Council.

The endowment of the Boys' School is derived from the profits of certain lands and tenements bequeathed to the Corporation, in the reign of Henry VI. (1442), by one John Carpenter, then Town Clerk of London. The bequest was "for the finding and bringing up of foure poore men's children, with meate, drinke, apparell, learning at the Schooles, in the Universities, etc., until they be preferred, and then others in their places, for ever." From time to time various schemes were framed extending the educational benefits conferred by the bequest. On the 18th January, 1832, the Court of Common Council resolved that, at an annual cost of £420, four boys from eight to sixteen years of age, sons of Freemen (to be nominated from time to time by the Lord Mayor), should be sent for education and maintenance to the Skinners' School at Tonbridge. In the year 1834, the Corporation applied to Parliament for leave to discontinue one of its Markets, called Honey Lane Market, in Milk Street, Cheapside, and to erect on the site of the same a School for the education of boys. On the 13th August, in the same year, an Act was passed discontinuing Honey Lane Market, and authorising the Corporation to erect the proposed school on the site thereof, such school to be for ever thereafter maintained by the Corporation "for the religious and virtuous education of boys and for instructing them in the higher branches of literature and all other useful learning."

The School was completed and opened for work on the 2nd of February, 1837, when upwards of 400 pupils assembled, and a career of success was commenced which has since been not only maintained, but has steadily augmented. The site proving too confined for extension, it was resolved by the Court of Common Council, on the 4th November 1878, to remove the School to land belonging to the Corporation, on the Victoria Embankment, notwithstanding its great value—upwards of £100,000. Accordingly, the Corporation procured the passing of the City of London School Act, 1879, under the powers of which statute, the Corporation, at an expenditure of about £100,000, erected the present School buildings. On the 12th of December, 1882, the new School was opened by H.R.H. the Prince of Wales, Alderman Sir H. E. Knight (an old boy of the School) being then Lord Mayor.

During the existence of the School, various benevolent persons, and some of the City Guilds, have presented Donations and Scholarships to the value of £1,792 10s. 6d. a year, besides which books and medal prizes, worth about £200 a year, are annually given to the boys. The number of Scholarships in connection with the School is 49, tenable at Oxford or Cambridge, the London University, and the City of London School, eight of which are in memory of John Carpenter, the original founder of the School. The School is divided into three sides, Classical, Modern, and Scientific. Boys are admitted at any age between 7 and 15 years, and may remain until the age of 19; or longer, by permission of the School Committee. The present number on the books is 700. The charge for each pupil is £15 15s. a year. The mode of admission (as also for the Girls' School) is on the nomination of an Alderman or Common Councilman, subject to examination by the Head Master. The receipts from fees are about £11,200 a year, which the Corporation supplements by annual grants out of the City's Cash, amounting, on an average, to £4,000 per annum. Between the years 1835 and 1898, the Corporation has expended a total sum upon this School (including the value of the site) of over £350,000.

The City of London School for Girls is the outcome of the bequest of the late Mr. William Ward of Brixton, who in 1881, left to the Corporation of London the sum of £20,000 for the establishment of a School for Girls, corresponding as nearly as possible to the City of London School for Boys. The School was opened in September, 1894, and cost nearly £19,000, exclusive of the site, which was valued at £10,000. The work is of a high standard, and is now being carried on in the various branches of instruction included in the School curriculum. The School at present, possesses eight Scholarships, seven of which, amounting to the value of £150, are tenable in the School, and one of the value of £50 a year is tenable at a college for the higher instruction of women. Girls are admissible from seven years of age, and may remain, by permission of the School Committee, until 19, or longer. There are now 150 pupils. The charge for each pupil is £9 9s. a year under 10, and over that age £12 12s. a year.

The annual grant out of City's cash since the opening of the School, has amounted to nearly £1,000.

THE MUSIC COMMITTEE.

The Music Committee is entrusted with the general management and control of the Guildhall School of Music, on the Thames Embankment, including the engagement of the Professors, numbering about 120, who are paid by the fees of pupils, which amount to some thousands of pounds per annum. The Court of Common Council makes an annual average grant of about 2,000 guineas towards the support of the School. It was founded in 1879 as the Guildhall Orchestral Society, and was permitted to occupy a large warehouse in Aldermanbury, the property of the Corporation. It immediately became popular, and under the fostering care of the Corporation, grew so rapidly that it was soon found to be necessary to obtain greater accommodation, which resulted in the erection, in 1886, of the handsome building on the Victoria Embankment, at a cost of nearly £27,000. The advantages offered to the public of the Metropolis in obtaining a thorough musical education have been so much appreciated, that extensive additions to the building became imperative. In 1897, the Court of Common Council approved the plans (which included a theatre, with seating accommodation for 740 persons) of the City Surveyor for the erection of a building in communication with that erected in 1886. This annexe was opened in July, 1898, and cost, including furnishing, £21,000. There are at present 3,600 students attending the School. Admission is on the nomination of an Alderman or a member of the Court of Common Council.

The Principal, Secretary, and Lady Superintendent of the School are in the appointment of the Court of Common Council ; the two former being annually elected.

THE FREEMEN'S ORPHAN SCHOOL COMMITTEE.

This Committee has the entire management of the affairs of the City of London Freemen's Orphan School, save the election of the children, who are balloted for by the whole Court. It has the appointment of all the School Officers, with the exception of the Head-Master, who is appointed by the Court of Common Council.

This School was erected by the Corporation, and opened in the year 1854 under the authority of the Freemen's Orphan School Act of that year and was established " for the maintenance and the religious and virtuous education of Orphans of Freemen of the City of London." The School is partially supported by the rents of freehold estates, devised in former times by charitable persons connected with the Corporation of the City of London, but its principal source of income is City's cash. The average annual cost to the Corporation is £6,000. The number of children in the School was originally fixed at 100, viz. : 65 boys and 35 girls; but this number was increased in 1863 to 150, viz., 100 boys and 50 girls ; the number now maintained is 100 boys and 65 girls. Up to the present time, some 970 children have passed through the School, viz., 624 boys and 346 girls. The children are admitted between the ages of 7 and 10, and remain in the School until the age of 15, two boys and two girls (selected for their good conduct and ability) being allowed to remain a year longer as pupil teachers. On leaving the School each child is provided with an outfit ; and those who are meritorious, and make application, are apprenticed to suitable trades.

The cost of the buildings with additions has been £30,000 and the annual grants have amounted to £190,000.

OPEN SPACES.

THE EPPING FOREST COMMITTEE.

This Committee has the control of Epping Forest, Wanstead Park, and Higham Park, which contain altogether 5,559 acres, which have been acquired at an expense to the Corporation of £290,087, and involve an annual charge for maintenance of about £4,000.

By the Epping Forest Act, 1878, the Forest is to be regulated and managed by the Corporation of London, acting by the Court of Common Council, as the Conservators of the Forest. For the purposes of management, the Statute provides that a committee shall be appointed, to be styled The Epping Forest Committee, which Committee is to have authority to exercise those powers which the Conservators are authorised to exercise under the Act, and the Court of Common Council is empowered from time to time to select a number, not exceeding twelve of their members, to be members of The Epping Forest Committee. The four Verderers (who are elected by the Commoners in pursuance of the Act), are also to be members of the Committee, and have the same powers as those members who are chosen from the Court of Common Council. The acts and proceedings of the Committee are, by the Statute, to be done and conducted according to the same rules and practice as if the Committee were a Committee of the Court of Common Council. The Verderers are elected for seven years, but casual vacancies are filled up by the Conservators from among persons qualified to be elected Verderers.

Under the Act, the Committee acquires numerous and extensive powers of managing the Forest, and power is given to make bye-laws for the protection of the Forest, the prevention of nuisances, and the preservation of order ; such bye-laws are to be allowed by the Ranger of the Forest, acting with the advice and assistance of the First Commissioner of Works. The Conservators are also, to provide and maintain offices in the Forest and elsewhere as they think fit for the transaction of business, and they may employ the Officers of the Corporation, or from time to time, with the approval of the ·Ranger, appoint a treasurer and other officers and servants and pay them such fees and salaries, and grant them such pensions and retiring allowances as they think fit.

The Committee of Managers of West Ham·Park.

This Committee is composed of 15 members, eight of whom are appointed by the Court of Common Council, four by the representatives of the late Mr. Gurney, who was the vendor of the Park to the Corporation. This right was conceded to him in consideration of his having sold the Park for considerably less than its market value. The remaining three Members of the Committee are appointed by the Parish of West Ham. The Park was acquired by a voluntary agreement with Mr. Gurney in 1874, the Corporation obtaining a license in mortmain to enable them to hold it. The Bye-laws for its regulation were made under the City of London Various Powers Act, 1877. West Ham Park contains 77 acres, and has cost the Corporation over £20,000, and a present annual expenditure of about £1,500.

Under the control of the Coal and Corn and Finance Committee are the following *Open Spaces*, which have been acquired by the Corporation.

Burnham Beeches.

The 'Beeches' are 375 acres in extent, and have been described as "a wild woodland tract of great beauty." They are situated four miles from Slough on the Great Western Railway. This was the first open space acquired by the Corporation (in 1883) under their Act of 1878, and cost £10,000, in addition to an annual charge for maintenance of nearly £500.

COULSDON COMMONS.

These Commons are near Caterham in Surrey, and contain nearly 350 acres, and comprise portions of Riddlesdown, Kenley, Farthing Downs and Coulsdon Commons. They were acquired in 1883 at a cost to the Corporation of upwards of £7,000. In addition to which there is an annual charge for maintenance of about £200.

HIGHGATE WOOD AND QUEEN'S PARK.

The combined area of the above open spaces is nearly 100 acres, and the cost to the Corporation has been over £6,000. The cost of maintenance is over £1,000 per annum. Opened 1886.

ST. PAUL'S CHURCHYARD.

This open space was thrown open to the public in 1879, and cost the Corporation £5,600. It is now maintained by it out of its own funds, at an annual expense of £350.

ADMINISTRATION.
THE MARKETS COMMITTEE.

The management and supervision of the City Markets are entrusted to three different Committees, viz., the Billingsgate and Leadenhall Markets, the Central Markets, and the Cattle Markets Committees. The Market rights and privileges of the Corporation of London originated in very remote times. Markets have been in existence in the City of London for more than 1,000 years, and the Corporation has for many centuries been the Market Authority for London.

The existing Corporation Markets are :—

Billingsgate Market.
London Central Markets at Smithfield.
Metropolitan Cattle Market at Islington.
Foreign Cattle Market at Deptford.
Leadenhall Market, and
Smithfield Hay Market.

BILLINGSGATE MARKET.

Billingsgate is the most ancient market belonging to the Corporation, and is situated by the water-side in Lower Thames Street. It was used for the sale of fish 1,000 years ago, and has from time to time been enlarged and extended. During the last 50 years, over £300,000 has been expended for that purpose.

The deliveries at the Market have been as under :—

		By Land.		By Water.		Total Tons.
1895	..	89,854	..	37,437	..	127,291
1896	..	95,278	..	42,884	..	138,162
1897	..	90,213	..	49,014	..	139,227
1898	..	94,535	..	52,778	..	147,313

LEADENHALL MARKET.

The supplies at Leadenhall Market cannot be given, as, no toll being levied, the weight is not ascertained.

LONDON CENTRAL MARKETS.

These stand partly on the site of Old Smithfield Market, and comprise the following Markets and Sections :—

London Central Meat Market.

London Central Poultry and Provision Market.

London Central General Market, comprising

Poultry and Provision Section,

Inland Fish Section,

Fruit, Vegetable and Flower Section.

The latter section was founded on the disestablishment of Farringdon Market in 1892. The first of these Markets was opened in 1868, and is believed to be at the present time the largest dead meat market in existence.

The deliveries for the first year, 1869, were 127,981 tons, and for last year, 1898, 405,282 tons. The aggregate total for last year is made up as follows :—

Country killed meat	..	..	..	..	112,705	tons.
Town killed	..	..	..	..	..	79,784	,,
European	..	..	..	..	..	51,122	,,
American	..	..	..	..	..	77,104	,,
Australian and New Zealand	..	..	..	84,567	,,

These Markets afford employment, directly and indirectly, to about 9,000 persons.

The capital expended on the Central Markets has been about two millions.

SMITHFIELD HAY MARKET.

For many centuries prior to the establishment of the Metropolitan Cattle Market at Islington, a Hay Market, as well as a Market for the sale of cattle, sheep, and horses, was held in Smithfield under the management and control of the Corporation. The Cattle Market was removed to Islington in 1855, under an Act of Parliament, but the Hay Market was not included, and has continued to be held at Smithfield on a site specially reserved for the purpose by the Metropolitan Meat and Poultry Market Act of 1860.

The charge is 6d. a load on all hay and straw sold, and a public register is provided showing all such sales.

METROPOLITAN CATTLE MARKET, ISLINGTON.

This Market was formerly held at Smithfield, and was removed to its present site in 1855, under the powers of the Metropolitan Market Act, 1851.

The capital outlay has amounted to half a million.

The following are the Returns :—

1895	..	..	..	919,349 animals.
1896	..	..	..	798,445 ,,
1897	..	..	..	739,534 ,,
1898	..	..	..	682,838 ,,

Extensive lairage and commodious slaughterhouses are provided. The Market finds employment for some 1,600 persons. There are two blocks of model dwellings within the market area, accommodating 124 families.

FOREIGN CATTLE MARKET, DEPTFORD.

Under the Contagious Diseases (Animals) Act, 1869, the Corporation of the City of London was made the exclusive local authority for the purposes of that Act, in and for the Metropolis, subject to its providing and opening for public use a market before the 1st January, 1872, and on that day this market was duly opened. It has since been enlarged, and now covers about 30 acres, occupies the site of the old Admiralty Dockyard, and has a river frontage of about 1,050 feet.

The total outlay for site and construction has been about £430,000. The business of this market is liable to the most serious fluctuation in the event of the outbreak abroad of cattle disease.

The number of animals landed in 1897 was 223,628 cattle and 286,990 sheep ; in 1898, 224,993 cattle, 353,095 sheep, 408 pigs.

From the opening of the market in 1872 to the close of 1898, 13,804,125 animals have been landed from 22,266 steamers and slaughtered at the market, chiefly for the food supply of the Metropolis.

For the convenience of shipowners, and to avoid the necessity for their largest ships discharging at the market jetties, three commodious steam vessels have been provided and specially fitted for daily use in trans-shipping animals in the river or docks, and conveying them to the market. Since the commencement of this service in 1879, 1,001,541 cattle and 152,652 sheep have been so landed at the market.

In 1879, 28,653 Cattle arrived from the United States of America.
,, 1889, 99,842 ,, ,, ,, ,, ,,
,, 1897, 144,679 ,, ,, ,, ,, ,,
,, 1898, 133,422 ,, ,, ,, ,, ,,
,, 1890, 22 Cattle and 3,075 Sheep from the River Plate (Argentina).
,, 1892, 99 ,, 976 ,, ,, ,, ,,
,, 1894, 4,971 ,, 36,564 ,, ,, ,, ,,
,, 1897, 49,584 ,, 248,037 ,, ,, ,, ,,
,, 1898, 66,769 ,, 324,680 ,, ,, ,, ,,

Three jetties run 160 feet into the river, and vessels ranging from 1,000 to 6,500 tons are discharged, frequently three or more on one tide.

Railway accommodation and other works are now in hand at a further estimated cost of £105,000.

There is covered lairage accommodation for 7,700 beasts, and 16,000 sheep, accommodation for slaughtering 2,600 beasts, and 4,000 sheep per day, chill room accommodation for 2,200 sides of beef, every 24 hours. Many of the larger slaughterhouses have also cooling rooms attached. Animals are sold alive chiefly to wholesale butchers, and slaughtered by them within 10 days of their arrival, in accordance with the orders of the Board of Agriculture. Accommodation is provided for cleaning and cooking the edible offal, and for other purposes. The offal of a bullock furnishes a meal for about 60 persons, and that of a sheep for eight. In the business of the market and its connections, probably not less than 2,500 hands are employed daily.

Speaking generally, all the Corporation markets have been either built, reconstructed, or enlarged within the last 50 years, and the Corporation, as the owner and the market authority, has maintained and managed all the markets under its control for the benefit of the whole of the Metropolis, without any rate being levied upon the inhabitants of the City or Metropolis ; and at the present day it may be fairly said that the series of markets for the convenience of the people of London is unequalled in size and utility throughout the world.

The entire capital sum expended by the Corporation on its markets may be approximately given at £4,000,000.

THE CITY POLICE COMMITTEE.

This Committee is the largest Committee of the Corporation, and consists of the Lord Mayor, all the Aldermen, the Deputies and 29 Commoners.

The Committee appoints the Surgeon and Receiver, and carries the various Acts relating to the City Police into execution (except as to the disciplinary portion, which is under the control of the Commissioner), has the general manage-

ment and control of all the buildings in the occupation of the
Force, Police Stations, Hospital, &c., and provides all the
necessary accoutrements. The City Police Force is under the
command of a Commissioner, and consists of about 1,000 officers
and men. The expenses (about £135,000 per annum) are met by
a contribution from the City's Cash of one-fourth part, and the
remainder by a rate levied in the several Wards of the City.
The following account of the origin and rise of the Force may
prove interesting :—

From time immemorial, the citizens of London have had
the control of their own Police, anciently called The Watch,
and this, indeed, was one of their most cherished rights and
privileges. As far back as history goes, the care and control of
the Police of the City have always been in the hands of the
citizens, either through the medium of the Train Bands,
through the Watch and Ward Committee, or otherwise ; this
was originally effected by causing every Inhabitant of a Ward
to take a personal share in the duties of "Watch and Ward."
In 1693, an Act of Common Council was passed which provided
that more than 1,000 Watchmen should be constantly on duty
in the City from sunset to sunrise, and that every inhabitant
should take his turn. This was called the "Standing Watch."
There had also been established, from a very early period, for
extraordinary occasions, a body called the "Marching Watch,"
which was mustered regularly at Midsummer, under the
Mayor and Sheriffs, until the early part of the reign
of Edward VI., when it was put down on account of
its having caused excessive expenditure. In later times,
peace and order were secured in the City by the supervision of City Marshals, under whose care the City Day
Watch was placed. In 1737, the Night Watch of the City
was regulated by an Act of Parliament "for better regulating
the Night Watch and Bedels within the City of London and
Liberties thereof, and for making more effectual the Laws now

in being, for paving and cleansing the streets and sewers in and about the said City."

Under this Act, a more efficient system of Police was established by day, as well as by night. This Police Force was superintended by the Aldermen, and then consisted of 68 men. It was subsequently found to be insufficient, and was, consequently, re-modelled by the Lord Mayor and Aldermen, in April, 1832, in which form it existed up to 1839. The Force then consisted of 99 men.

When the Metropolitan Police Force was first established by the late Sir Robert Peel, he took the City Police, as then existing, for his model. He, however, desired to consolidate the two Forces, but the Corporation strongly objected to this, and advanced four principal reasons for keeping them distinct, viz. : 1st.—" That the City so differs in its locality " and the nature of its property from other parts of the " Metropolis as to require a separate and differently regulated " Police Force for its protection." 2nd.—" That it would be " a great inconvenience to the inhabitants of the City to be " obliged to apply to the Commissioners at Whitehall, in cases " of complaint against constables." 3rd.—" That the taking " away the power of appointing and managing its own Police " would be an interference with the Charters and Privileges " of the City." 4th.—" That the inhabitants would sustain " a great pecuniary loss by being deprived of the contribution " which is now made from the Corporation Funds towards " the expense of the City Police." These reasons prevailed. The Corporation and the citizens maintained their old constitutional right of self-government, and the City remained undisturbed in its ancient right and privilege of " Watch and Ward." The Corporation introduced a Bill into Parliament in the then Session (1839) for the regulation of their own Police, preserving all their rights and privileges.

This led to the Act of that year being passed for regulating the Police in the City of London, under which the Force is now managed.

Many testimonies to the good management of the City Police have not prevented attempts to deprive the City of the management of its own force. One of the attempts led to a remarkable requisition from upwards of 3,000 Merchants, Bankers, and Citizens (headed by the late Baron Lionel de Rothschild), calling for a Meeting in Guildhall to consider the question with a view to protesting against the proposed interference. A Meeting was consequently held on May 5th, 1863, when the following Resolution was proposed by the Governor of the Bank of England :—

" That the citizens of London obtained from the Sovereigns " of these realms the right of electing their own Magistrates, " and of keeping watch and ward within the City, a right which " has ever been exercised for the benefit of the people and the " protection of their liberties; that the Bill for the Amalgamation " of the City of London Police with the Metropolitan Police is " an invasion of this right, and is subversive of the old English " Constitutional principle of Local Self-Government, which has " fostered the love of freedom in this country, has drawn closer " the ties which connect the people with the Crown and " Parliament, and under which this City and the Nation " at large have so long prospered." The Resolution was carried, and the Bill for the deprivation of the City's rights withdrawn.

The City, notwithstanding the enormous value of the property within its area, is, by night, practically deserted by the three or four hundred thousand of its day population, who are content to leave the protection of their possessions to the City Police Force—a most eloquent testimony to its entire and absolute efficiency. Lord Mayor Phillips (1897) justly described the City Police as "The most civil and the best civil force in the world."

THE COUNTY PURPOSES COMMITTEE.

This Committee has most important functions to discharge, mainly in consequence of the passing of the Local Government Act, 1888, by which were transferred to the Mayor, Commonalty, and Citizens of the City, acting by the Court of Common Council, various powers, duties, and liabilities of the Corporation, then hitherto acting by the Court of Aldermen, or by the Court of Quarter Sessions. Among the duties so transferred, were those arising under the following statutes :—

The Explosives Act, 1875 ; The Weights and Measures Act, 1878 ; The Petroleum Acts, 1871 and 1879 ; The Reformatory and Industrial Schools Acts ; Shop Hours Act, 1892 ; the Acts relating to Pauper Lunatic Asylums, so far as regards the Provision, Enlargement, Maintenance, Management, and Visitation of the City of London Lunatic Asylum at Stone. Under the Lunacy Act, 1890, the Court of Common Council was appointed the Local Authority for the City of London ; the control and management of the Asylum now rest with the Visiting Committee, consisting of twelve Members nominated by the County Purposes Committee and elected by the Court of Common Council, as such Local Authority. A further power transferred to the Court of Common Council by the Local Government Act, 1888, was that of making a County Rate, which would be applicable to the payment of the following :—Debts incurred in respect of Lunatic Asylums and Industrial Schools ; Pensions in connection with Prison Officials ; Expenses in connection with the recovery of Drowned Bodies, Registration of Voters, Pauper Lunatics, Industrial Schools,

N

Coroner, Administration of Justice (Central Criminal Court), including the provision and maintenance of Courts and Offices.

THE CITY OF LONDON LUNATIC ASYLUM

was erected during the years 1863, 1864, and 1865, under the direction of the Special Asylum Committee of the Court of Common Council, from plans prepared by James Bunstone Bunning, Esq., the then City Architect, and was opened for the reception of patients on the 16th April, 1866. The original accommodation was for 125 of either sex. The estate comprised 33 acres, which has since been enlarged to 140 acres, a large portion of which is used as a farm, which is of invaluable assistance in providing healthy labour and recreation for the inmates, at the same time supplying the patients with fresh and wholesome food.

The style of the building is Tudor ; it is arranged upon the corridor principle, which, thirty years ago, was thought to be the most suitable for these Institutions. Since 1866, many additions have been made, notably in 1874, 1878, and 1885, when an extension and spur to the female wing were added, a detached Hospital for infectious cases erected, and the male wing extended. Extensive additions and improvements are now in progress, at an estimated cost of about £85,000. The total expenditure from the City's Cash for the purchase of land, erection and maintenance of buildings, has been upwards of £123,000. The City's Cash also contributes upwards of £1,100 per annum for the maintenance of patients, for whom no legal settlements can be found. There are, at present, in residence 472 patients (222 males and 250 females), of these, 393 belong to the pauper class and 79 are private, their relatives paying a Guinea a week for their maintenance. The latter accommodation is much appreciated, and there is always a long list of patients waiting for admission. The recovery rate for the past quinquennial period, has been considerably above the average recovery rate for the County and Borough Asylums, and the death rate for this period, has been one of the lowest in England. Ample out-door employment, and a healthy site, have largely contributed thereto.

The late Lord Mayor, Lieut.-Col. Sir Horatio David Davies, K.C.M.G., M.P., is Chairman of the Committee.

THE PORT OF LONDON SANITARY COMMITTEE.

The work of the Port of London Sanitary Committee properly comes under the head of Public Health, but it is placed in its present position, for the reason that the whole of the expenses attendant in carrying on the duties assigned to it are discharged by the Corporation out of its own Funds, and not out of the Rates, as are all the expenses in carrying on the work of the Health Department.

This Committee was originally appointed in 1873, and has since been annually re-appointed, under the various Public Health Acts. To it is delegated the duty of carrying into execution the powers of the Corporation, as the Port Sanitary Authority for the Port of London. The Committee has the management of the Port Sanitary Hospital, at Denton, near Gravesend, and the dealing (through their medical officers) with all cases of infectious disease brought into the Port of London by any vessels.

During the year 1898, by means of the system of medical inspection, as carried out by the Medical Officers of the Authority, 79 cases of infectious disease were removed from vessels and dealt with at the entrance of the port.

The total number of ships thus visited by the Medical Officers on arrival from foreign ports during the year was 10,332. Of these 1,096 were medically inspected, this involving individual examination of 5,789 passengers, and 14,279 persons forming the crews of such vessels.

A similar system is carried out by the Authority at Sheerness, the estuary of the Medway coming within the limits of the Port of London. At this station 167 vessels were visited by the Medical Officer stationed there. In addition to the medical inspection, sanitary inspection of vessels is carried out throughout the docks and port generally by a staff of nine inspectors. In this way, during the year 1898, 31,658 vessels were inspected.

The inspection of food brought into the port from abroad also constitutes an important branch of the work of the Sanitary Authority, and considerable quantities of unsound food stuffs of all kinds, including meat, fruit, fish, etc., are seized and destroyed annually by the officers specially appointed for the purpose.

The sanitary inspection of vessels not only involves the duty of seeing that the crews' quarters are kept clean, but also the carrying out of such structural alterations as may be necessary for the improvement of the sanitary condition of these places ; and during the year under review 591 alterations of this class, affecting 537 vessels, were effected.

For the purposes of sanitary inspection in the River, and removal of cases of infectious disease, the Authority maintains three steam launches in constant work. These launches patrol the whole of the district which extends from Teddington Lock to about five miles below the Nore, and embraces all waterways within these limits, including the whole of the Docks.

The offices of the Authority are situated at Greenwich, and are in charge of the Medical Officer of Health. who, as the chief executive officer, is responsible for the proper working of the various departments, including the Infectious Hospital above referred to, and the staff of medical officers stationed at Gravesend and Sheerness.

In the month of February, 1893, with a view to the consideration of the best measures for the prevention of the introduction of Cholera into this country, and promoting unity of action among Sanitary Authorities, the Committee initiated, and with the consent of the Court of Common Council, held, on the 17th day of that month, a Conference of Port Sanitary Authorities of England and Wales, which was presided over by the Lord Mayor, and attended by 108 delegates, representing 41 Authorities. Important resolutions, dealing with hospitals, inspection of vessels, disinfection, and kindred matters, were discussed and passed, and forwarded to the Local Government Board, the President of which, in his place in the House of Commons, bore testimony to the work of the Committee in the following words: "I think the Port " Sanitary Authority of London is pre-eminently distinguished " for the admirable manner in which it has discharged its " duty."

The amount spent by the Committee, on behalf of the Corporation, in safeguarding the health of the Port of London, has amounted, for the 25 years during which the duties have been carried out, to no less than £126,000. The average annual amount expended during the last three years being £7,000.

The cost of the work carried out by the different Committees of the Court of Common Council, as described in the foregoing pages, is entirely borne by the City's Cash, that is to say, the produce of the estates of the Corporation, and without the levying of any rate upon the citizens, with the exception of three-fourths of the expenses of the City Police Force (under the Act of 1839), as noted on page 190.

An exceedingly important section of the work carried on by the Court of Common Council is that of

THE PUBLIC HEALTH DEPARTMENT.

This Department of the Corporation carries on the work performed by the late Commission of Sewers, which body was merged into the Corporation by the City of London Sewers Act, 1897, which came into operation on the 10th January, 1898. The original Commission, as constituted at the time of its dissolution, was created in the year following the Great Fire of London (1666) by an Act of Parliament, entitled, "An Act for Re-building the City of London." From the time of its institution to its dissolution it had always been composed of Members of the Corporation, with the Lord Mayor at its head.

It is somewhat difficult in a limited space to detail the multifarious duties appertaining to this branch of the Corporation, or to give an adequate idea of the scope of its work, which is carried on by the means of four Committees, each reporting, like all other Committees of the Corporation, to the Court of Common Council, viz. :—

> The Improvements and Finance Committee,
> The Streets Committee,
> The Sanitary Committee,
> The Accounts Committee.

The due administration of the work, which is carried out under upwards of thirty Acts of Parliament (see page 206), involves the employment of a regular staff of some nine hundred persons, and an outlay in 1898 of about £549,000. Of this sum, £149,000 is in respect of the repayment of instalments and interest on loans for improvements of the public streets, and £267,000 to meet the Precepts of the London School

Board. The total debt on loans at the commencement of the year was £1,337,983, which is annually decreasing to the extent of £67,000, in addition to provision made by Sinking Funds for meeting Bonds maturing in particular years.

The Corporation, under the City of London Sewers Acts, has rating powers for the purposes of the Public Health Department, in respect of the Sewer Rate of 4d. in the £, and of the Consolidated Rate of 1s. 6d. in the £. The rates for the current year being only 1d. and 1s. 2½d. in the £ respectively, there is thus a larger margin of rating power available. It also has rating powers for special purposes, under other Acts, such as the Education Act, (the total amount collected by the late Commission for School Board Purposes exceeded £3,000,000), and Dwelling-House Improvement Acts, under which the Commission erected Artizans' Dwellings in Stoney Lane accommodating 1,000 persons.

THE OFFICERS OF THE "PUBLIC HEALTH DEPARTMENT."

The Town Clerk is head of the Department, under whom all the other officers act.

The Heads of Departments are the Principal Clerk, the Medical Officer of Health and Food Analyst, the Engineer, and the Superintendent of Cleansing, &c.

THE PRINCIPAL CLERK

has an important and responsible position. He has to attend the Courts of Common Council, whilst matters affecting the Public Health Department are under discussion, and all Committees of the Department, and is responsible for the proper conduct of the whole of the business, as well as for the correctness of the accounts. He is Clerk of the City of London Burial Board, and has control of all matters in connection with the City of London Cemetery at Ilford.

The Medical Officer of Health and Food Analyst.

The duties of the Medical Officer of Health for the City of London are defined by the provisions of the City of London Sewers Acts, 1848 and 1851, the Public Health Act, 1891, and by the various Acts of Parliament having reference to, or for regulating, the sanitary condition of the City of London, and include such other duties as may be imposed by any Act of Parliament, or by any orders or regulations, having reference to sanitary matters, made by the Corporation.

The duties of the Food Analyst are defined by the Adulteration of Food and Drugs Acts.

The Engineer.

The duties of the Engineer consist, principally, in the supervision of all works connected with the Public Lighting, Paving, Sewerage, &c., of the City of London. All accounts for these works are examined, checked and certified by him. He has to prepare all plans and estimates for the widening and improvement of the City Streets, and conducts all negotiations for the acquisition of the properties required, and the disposal of the surplus lands and buildings that remain. He designs and superintends the construction of the various public conveniences that have been placed beneath the public ways in the City of London. All plans of House Drains, and the construction of house drains beneath the public ways, and the interiors of buildings are under his control. The Subways (in which are hydraulic mains, gas and water pipes, electric wires, &c.) beneath the public ways are also under his control.

The Superintendent of Cleansing, Dusting and Watering.

The duties of the Superintendent of Cleansing require him to devote himself to his work by night, as well as by day, and, if needful, on Sundays as well as on week days, as the necessities of the public service may require. It is his business to keep the Streets in a perfect state of cleanliness, and to see that refuse of all descriptions is removed from the City as promptly as possible ; to engage and discharge all hands, to define their duties, arrange the hours of working, and from time to time make such alterations in their wages as are needed.

THE IMPROVEMENTS AND FINANCE COMMITTEE.

Upon this Committee, as its name denotes, devolve all questions of improvements in the public streets. The net expenditure by the late Commission of Sewers in this matter alone during the past half century was about £2,500,000, exclusive of the contributions by the late Metropolitan Board of Works, the London County Council, and the City's Cash, the result being that every important street in the City has been improved and widened, and the congestion of traffic at many points greatly relieved, notably in the cases of Ludgate Hill, Poultry, Monument Street, East-cheap, Blomfield Street, &c., &c. At the present moment, the much needed widening of Fleet Street, and also of Cheapside (west end) is well in hand.

Many of the main thoroughfares, thus improved, have greatly benefited not only the City, but the whole of the, Metropolis. In the year 1898 over £140,000 was expended in acquiring properties for street improvements. Most of this work has been and is now carried out under the powers of the Act of 57th Geo. III., Cap. 29, commonly known as Michael Angelo Taylor's Act. This Committee is also responsible for the financial condition of the Department, and the correct annual statement of Assets and Liabilities, upon which the Rates needed for the current year are based and made.

It has also under its control the collection of the
Consolidated and Sewers Rates and all matters relating
thereto. The Parliamentary business affecting the Public Health
Department, is also dealt with principally by this Committee.

THE STREETS COMMITTEE.

This Committee has the management of all questions
relating to the paving and lighting of the Public Streets.
The cost of lighting with gas and electricity is £20,000 a
year, the annual cost of each arc lamp being £26. Asphalte,
wood, and stone paving cost £34,000, and cleansing, removal
of dust, and watering the streets £41,000 a year. Under
its control is the ever increasing work of the Cleansing
Department, which provides for the collection and disposal
of all dust and refuse within the City. The quantity of
street sweepings and dust removed annually is now about
80,000 tons : 30 years ago it was only 49,400.

In connection with this work there are three Depôts,
viz. :—at Letts' Wharf, Commercial Road, Upper Thames
Street (where the Superintendent of Cleansing resides) and the
Depôt in Stoney Lane. The dust and refuse removed from the
City is dealt with at Letts' Wharf (a revenue of £3,000 a
year is derived from the sale of string, cardboard, paper and
bottles, &c.), where the late Commission of Sewers erected Dust
Destructors, and all the necessary appliances for dealing
with refuse, as well as ranges of stables for the accommodation of the City stud, comprising about one hundred horses.
At this Depôt, the carts and wagons used for the removal
of the dust, etc., are made, as well as the harness,
horse-shoes, etc., and the horses are shod by farriers in the
employ of the Department. The cost of the Buildings
exceeded £88,000.

The Committee is also from time to time engaged in
protecting the interests of the public, in connection with any

Railway or other kindred works beneath the public way (as in the case of the Central London Railway and other works now in progress within the City area).

There are fifty miles of streets, lanes and courts in the City which require the close attention of this Committee. The quantity of water annually used for washing these streets, &c., is over 26,000,000 gallons, costing nearly £1,000. A recent day census taken showed that the number of vehicles passing through the streets in twenty-four hours was 92,372, and 1,186,094 pedestrians.

The Committee has under its control the Subways constructed by the Corporation under the Holborn Viaduct and in several new streets.

In addition to the above, the following works are supervised and dealt with by this Committee, viz. :—

Dangerous Structure Proceedings.

Construction and Maintenance of Public Conveniences. There are now nineteen of these structures in the City (some providing accommodation for women), and there are others in course of construction. The revenue derived from these places is about £6,000 a year.

Sewer Works. The length of sewers within the City, exclusive of the main sewers, which are under the management of the London County Council, is about 41 miles.

Water Supply, Artesian Well. Hoardings and Scaffolds.

Projecting Trade Tablets and Boards, &c.

All Projections over or upon the Public Way, such as Private Lamps, Vaults, Area Gratings, Coal Plates, etc.

The Sanitary Committee.

The Sanitary Committee is the Burial Board for the City of London, and is vested with all the powers of a Sanitary Authority in regard to the investigation of Zymotic Diseases, and the inspection of Lodging - Houses, Slaughter-Houses, Bake-Houses, Factories, Workshops, the Condemnation and Destruction of Diseased Meat, &c., the Removal of Nuisances, Suppression of Offensive Trades, Adulteration of Food, Smoke Nuisances, the Disinfection of Premises, &c. (after Contagious Diseases), and all other matters relating to the health of the community. In addition to this, a house-to-house visitation of the tenements of the City, is in daily progress.

Under the management of this Committee are the City of London Cemetery at Little Ilford, which was acquired and laid out by the late Commission of Sewers, in 1856, at a cost of about £82,000, the portion enclosed for the purposes of burial, being 118 acres, and there is a reserve of nearly 50 acres *(It is interesting to note that it was in consequence of this acquisition that the Corporation was enabled to sue the parties who had wrongfully possessed themselves of Forest land, and, eventually, through the action thus taken, that Epping Forest was preserved as an open space free to the public for ever)* also under the control of this Committee is the City Mortuary (containing a Chapel for the reception of dead bodies, a Post-Mortem Room, disinfecting apparatus of modern construction, Laboratories, Microscopical Room and a Coroner's Court), erected at a total outlay of about £12,000; and the Cotton Street Shelter in Cripplegate (for the temporary accommodation of families during the disinfection of their own homes).

THE ACCOUNTS COMMITTEE.

The Accounts Committee, (formed by the appointment of five members from each of the three before-mentioned Committees), is responsible for the examination and passing all Bills and Accounts before the same are finally presented for payment by the respective Committees.

They have also to examine and pass the periodical Disbursement Accounts of the various officers, and the accounts of the Collectors of Rates.

In concluding this short account of the work carried on by the Corporation in the government of the "one square mile," it can be asserted, without fear of contradiction, that, whether with respect to the Educational advantages offered to the general public, through the medium of its various Schools, or in the management of its Police, Markets and Open Spaces, or in the Lighting, Cleansing, Draining, and general Sanitary Work, or the Regulation of the enormous Vehicular and Pedestrian Traffic, and, in fact, by the completeness and the thorough efficiency of its Municipal Work, the City of London will bear favourable comparison with any City in the World. And it is by a due regard to the interests of the City ratepayers, that the large majority of the members of the Court are privileged, from year to year, to continue their labour of love and usefulness to the very great advantage of the citizens " of no mean City," and of the Metropolis at large.

Schedule of the principal Acts of Parliament under which the Corporation are or act as the Local Rating or Sanitary Authority.

Date of Act.	Chapter and Reign.	Title.
1817	57 Geo. III. c. xxix. ..	General Paving Act.
1848	11 & 12 Vict. c. clxiii. ..	City of London Sewers Act 1848.
1851	14 & 15 Vict. c. xci. ..	City of London Sewers Act 1851.
1852	15 & 16 Vict. c. 85 ..	The Burial Act 1852. .
1857	20 & 21 Vict. c. 35 ..	The City of London Burial Act 1857.
1867	30 & 31 Vict. c. 134 ..	The Metropolitan Streets Act 1867,
1869	32 & 33 Vict. c. 67 ..	The Valuation (Metropolis) Act 1869.
1871	34 & 35 Vict. c. cxxi. ..	The Wharves and Warehouses Steam Power and Hydraulic Pressure Company's Act 1871.
1875	38 & 39 Vict. c. 63 ..	Sale of Food and Drugs Act 1875.
1875	38 & 39 Vict. c. 83 ..	The Local Loans Act 1875
1875	38 Vict. c. iv.	The Commissioners of Sewers of the City of London Act 1875.
1878	41 Vict. c. 16	The Factory and Workshop Act 1878.
1879	42 & 43 Vict. c. 30 ..	Sale of Food and Drugs Act Amendment Act 1879.
1881	44 & 45 Vict. c. lxxxix...	The City of London Commissioners of Sewers (Artisans' Dwellings) Act 1881.
1881	44 & 45 Vict. c. 37 ..	Alkali &c. Works Regulation Act 1881.
1882	45 & 46 Vict. c. 56 ..	The Electric Lighting Act 1882.
1883	46 & 47 Vict. c. 53 ..	The Factory and Workshop Act 1883.
1884	47 & 48 Vict. c. lxxii. ..	The London Hydraulic Power Act 1884.
1887	50 & 51 Vict. c. 29 ..	The Margarine Act 1887.
1888	51 & 52 Vict. c. 12 ..	The Electric Lighting Act 1888.
1889	52 & 53 Vict. c. 11 ..	Sale of Horseflesh &c. Regulation Act 1889
1889	52 & 53 Vict. c. 27 ..	Advertising Stations (Rating) Act 1889.
1890	53 & 54 Vict. c. 70 ..	Housing of the Working Classes Act 1890.
1891	54 & 55 Vict. c. 76 ..	Public Health London Act 1891.
1891	54 & 55 Vict. c. lxxvii. ..	London Overhead Wires Act 1891.
1892	55 & 56 Vict. c. 30 ..	Alkali &c. Works Regulation Act 1892.
1892	55 & 56 Vict. c. 11 ..	Mortmain and Charitable Uses Act Amendment Act 1892.
1892	55 & 56 Vict. c. 57 ..	Private Street Works Act 1892.
1892	55 & 56 Vict. c. 59 ..	Telegraph Act 1892.
1892	55 & 56 Vict. c. lxxvii. ..	Corporation of London (Loans) Act 1892.
1894	57 & 58 Vict. c. 53 ..	London (Equalisation of Rates) Act 1894.
1894	57 & 58 Vict. c. ccxiii. ..	London Building Act 1894.
1895	58 & 59 Vict. c. 37 ..	Factory and Workshop Act 1895.

There are various other Acts of Parliament in which protective clauses have been inserted for the benefit of the Corporation.